THE BLOOD OF

JESUS

REVEALED

THE BLOOD OF JESUS REVEALED

APOSTLE D M LAKE

THE BLOOD OF JESUS REVEALED

Scripture quotations are taken from the King James version of the bible unless otherwise stated.

ISBN 0-9549243-2-0

Published by
Apostolic Publishing
22 Eastleigh Avenue
South Harrow
Middlesex UK
HA2 OUF

CONTENTS

DEDICATION

I would like to dedicate this book to my precious Lord and Saviour Jesus Christ, my all in all; to all of my wonderful children, their husbands and wives, my grandchildren and my great grandchildren. I would also like to further dedicate the book to all the ministers and saints of our ministry, the Apostolic Church of God 7th Day ministries at home and abroad.

You have all been so lovely and your love and kindness really encouraged me to go forward for the Lord.

God bless you all.

ACKNOWLEDGEMENT

I would like to acknowledge with all the thanks in the world, the love, mercy and kindness of my Lord and Saviour, Jesus Christ, in giving me revelation of the power in his blood. I used to mention the blood of Jesus at times. I knew that Jesus' blood paid the price for man's redemption, but I had no revelation of the depth of it.

In the first chapter of this book I will give my testimony of how the Lord began to reveal to me the power in his blood. Since then I have gone from victory to victory with more and deeper revelation as I go along.

The Lord spoke to me in clear tones: "I have given you the blood". I have taken it from the Lord and I use it for everything. I preach the blood of Jesus, I teach the blood of Jesus, I testify the blood of Jesus, I sing the blood of Jesus, I minister the blood of Jesus. I use the blood of Jesus against the strategies of satan and his cohorts and it works everytime.

In the spirit realm I walk the blood of Jesus, I talk the blood of Jesus, I drink the blood of Jesus, I sprinkle the blood of Jesus and I use the blood of Jesus by the Spirit of the Lord to cleanse people.

Teacher Max you not only minister with me in church, you support me as I minister the blood of Jesus on radio and television, and you do hear the many testimonies as people ring in to say how the Lord has delivered them from their destructions as I minister the blood of Jesus. Many who listen to the audio cassettes and video tapes have been healed.

I want to acknowledge, with thanks, the words you spoke to me Max. "You should write about the blood of Jesus". That went into my spirit and the Lord spoke to me and gave me the pattern for the book.

Sister Jacqui Johnson you have been a great help to me on the administrative and publishing side and may God forever bless you and yours.

Thanks again Ronnie for standing with me on the computer side with your expert advice. You were always willing and ready to help.

I also acknowledge with thanks the following:

Evangelist Fullerton for standing with me in ministry, day and night.

Evangelist Blake for being so faithful as we continue to Labour together for the Lord, ministering the blood on the radio.

Pastor Judy Fullerton, a very faithful daughter, friend and support worker in the office as we toiled together to get this work out.

Beloved Jonnie as you laboured with me ceaselessly on the computer with your wonderful knowledge when I didn't know how to proceed.

God bless you all.

INTRODUCTION

Revelation 12:11 And they overcame him by the blood of the Lamb and by the word of their testimony; and they loved not their lives unto the death.

The blood of Jesus is possibly the most powerful weapon for certain victory over the power of evil, if the believer will dare to avail himself of it in the name of Jesus.

In my early Christian walk, I occasionally heard ministers say that the blood of Jesus saved them. These words were spoken lightly. Until Jesus revealed the power of his blood to me, I cannot remember hearing a message preached on the blood of Jesus Christ. I believe the church has somewhere along the way either lost the understanding of the power in the blood of Jesus, or did not have it at all.

The Lord called me into ministry and for a few years we plodded along. I preached the word with power and prayed very much. Somehow, however, we did not seem to be moving forward as we should, and I kept asking the Lord why! The day came when the Lord answered my prayer in a way I would hardly have expected. I received revelation of the power in the blood of Jesus that would last me for the rest of my life. [I will give my testimony in Chapter 1 of this book]. Since then I have seen demons tremble and flee, diseases healed, problems solved, spirits of confusion disappear and at the sound of the blood of Jesus many souls have cried out for salvation.

I have taught our assemblies at home and abroad to plead the blood of Jesus. I have taught it on the radio, I have taught it on the television, and I am writing about it. I have taught the saints to drink [by faith] the blood of Jesus.

St John 6:54 Whoso eateth my flesh and drinketh my blood hath eternal life, and I will raise him up at the last day.

On the day the Lord worked that special miracle for me he said to me "I have given you the blood", and I have received it from the Lord. What God did that day was to open a major door into my understanding of the purpose of the blood of Jesus to the believer. I am receiving more revelation as the days go by.

Recently, whilst I was ministering the blood of Jesus on the radio, the Lord told me to tell his church to pour, by faith, the blood of Jesus over the building which is used for worship, sprinkle with the blood the podium, the bible on the podium, the musical instruments, all the bibles of the saints and sprinkle the people.

Exodus 24:6-10 6. And Moses took half of the blood and put it in basins and half of the blood he sprinkled on the altar. 7. And he took the book of the covenant and read in the audience of the people, and they said, All that the Lord hath said will we do and be obedient. 8. And Moses took the blood and sprinkled it on the people and said, Behold the blood of the covenant which the Lord hath made with you concerning all these words. 9. Then went up Moses and Aaron, Nadab and Abihu, and seventy of the elders of Israel. 10. And they saw the God of Israel and there was under his feet as it were a paved work of a sapphire stone, and as it were the body of heaven in his clearness.

When we pour out the blood on the people they will see God in his glory. The ministers will see God, the elders will see God. I told them to sound out the blood of Jesus: "the blood of Jesus, the blood of Jesus, the blood of Jesus", and walk around the assembly and pour out the blood in the name of Jesus.

As we ministered on the radio, there were so many testimonies coming in of what God was doing in the lives of the listeners as they pleaded the blood of Jesus, that our DJ, teacher Max said to me "Apostle Lake you should write a book on the blood of Jesus". As I waited in the presence of the Lord, he gave me the format for the book. To Jesus be all the glory and praise.

I have written in the hope that churches and ministries, in fact, all of God's people will have a fuller understanding of the power that is available to them when they use the blood of Jesus. Plead the blood for everything. I do, and our ministry is Holy Ghost fired up. The demons fear the blood. It has power to destroy them and the message to the enemies is loud and clear: "It is finished" [St John 19:30], the price has been paid, man has been liberated from the kingdom of darkness and Jesus Christ is Lord. The blood of Jesus must be given its rightful place in Christ's church. Plead the blood of Jesus and begin to read.

God bless you.

CHAPTER 1

HOW JESUS REVEALED TO ME THE POWER IN HIS BLOOD

Leviticus 17:11 For the life of the flesh is in the blood: and I have given it to you upon the altar to make an atonement for your souls; for it is the blood that maketh an atonement for the soul.

It was a very bleak and chilly day, winter lingered on. My son came in from work as usual, ready to take me shopping. "Conrad, I said, there is no need for you to take me shopping today, I will go to the local shop and ask them to deliver the shopping for me". "That's OK Mummy" he said, and I went off.

I had been living in the area for many years and normally I would meet up and talk with people known to me for a long time. However, it was fairly cold and I needed to go to the toilet so I did the shopping quickly, asked the shopkeeper to deliver and rushed home. When I got home, although I needed very much to go to the toilet, I had thought of stopping in the kitchen downstairs and of taking some fish out of the fridge that I had planned to cook that evening. The urgency of using the toilet prevented me from going into the kitchen and I ran upstairs.

My son was doing shift work at the time and he had a bath whenever he came in from work. I could smell the use of the bath . [The bath and the toilet were in the same room]. For years we had talked of putting another toilet downstairs but it never came to fruition. Thank God it didn't. Sometimes when things do not seem to be going the way we would like them to go, we should remember that all things work together for good to those who love the Lord. [Romans 8:28].

I knocked at the bathroom door, "open the door please" I said. I heard a groaning sound. "Are you constipated, open the door please". I was desperate. He undid the lock and I went into the bathroom. I had no plans for what I saw. My son was propped up against the wall, eyes closed. I thought he must have had a heart attack. I decided quickly to ring a Christian sister who was not working at the time and ask her to come and help whilst I call the doctor. A voice spoke to me very audibly, "there is no time for the doctor". God was on my case. I turned round quickly and the Holy Spirit took control. I grabbed hold of my son and cried out "Jesus help me, Lord you have to help me now". It was a loud cry of distress.
I felt the power of God overshadow me and I began to minister in the Lord's power. "Spirit of death, loose him, you can't have him, hand him over to me in Jesus' name". The words were being put in my mouth, they were definitely not rehearsed because I did not expect what I found. I began to plead the blood of Jesus very loudly, "the blood of Jesus, the blood of Jesus, the blood of Jesus". I pleaded the blood of Jesus until I began to say, "blood, blood, blood". The voice said to me "the blood of Jesus". Conrad stood on his feet. I began to say "Conrad, tell me what happened". The words had hardly left my mouth when he collapsed on me and his eyes closed. This was a tough spiritual battle the Lord was taking me through. I fought, using the blood of Jesus. I

pleaded the blood of Jesus with all my heart. The anointing was heavy on me; I felt like rain was falling on me. I took hold of Conrad's face and laid my hand on his forehead to pray for him, but as I did this, his face shook as though one was shaking fruits off a tree. Once again he stood upright but this time he was saying, "the blood of Jesus, the blood of Jesus, the blood of Jesus". I continued to plead the blood of Jesus, I was not taking any chances in case he slipped away again. I was making sure he had fully recovered.

As I continued to plead the blood of Jesus on the top of my voice, my son said, "Mummy, I am all right now".

"The blood of Jesus", I said. "Honestly, I am all right Mum". I continued pleading the blood of Jesus until I felt in my spirit that the Lord was through with the miracle he was performing.

I again said, "Conrad, tell me what happened" The bath was still full of water and he was naked. We let the water out, he put his clothes on, and here is the story:

After I had left the house to do the shopping, he went to have his usual bath. The bathroom was cold and the water for his bath was fairly hot. The bathroom was showing signs of condensation and he had opened the window to let the steam out. Whilst he was in the bath he was praying. He thought his ears were filling up with water and he leaned over to each side to shake any water out. Nothing came out of either ear. The vehicles passing near our home sounded miles away. Things did not seem normal. He said "Father what's happening here". He came out of the bath. By then his ears had completely blocked up. He saw what looked like a casket come from above and it covered him. The casket was transparent. He saw me come into the bathroom but the casket separated him from me and he was unable to communicate with me. He slipped out of his body at a very high speed and travelled upward so fast that by the time I started pleading the blood of Jesus he must have been thousands of miles out in space. I told Conrad I had been binding the spirit of death. He said the only words he heard were "the blood of Jesus". He said, "you stopped pleading the blood of Jesus at one time because I seemed to have travelled even faster when you stopped". I said, "it would have been the time when I thought you had come round".

Conrad said that at first, as I pleaded the blood of Jesus, he heard it very faintly and it began to pull him back. As he came back a bit closer to earth he heard it a little louder. He said, as I continued to plead the blood of Jesus it dragged him back step by step. It was like a cord pulling him back until it pulled him right back into his body.

"How did you get into the bathroom Mummy", he asked. I said, "you opened the door". "I couldn't have done", he said. "Well, the Holy Ghost did", I replied.

As I came back to myself I stood at the bathroom door wondering what had happened. The voice of the Lord spoke to me again "That is how you are to minister to Karen". Karen is my youngest daughter. She was in primary school at the time and had had an infection in her stomach. I was looking to the Lord to heal her. I had prayed for her many times over three weeks and it would not go. She screamed in pain day and night. She just cried when she came in from school. About three days before Conrad's miracle I rang the doctor and made an appointment to take Karen to see her. I reasoned that the Lord was not healing her as perhaps he wanted me to take her to the doctor so he could do something special that I had not seen before. She was in a lot of pain and I decided that it would not be fair on the child to wait any longer for a miracle.

The Lord was going to do a miracle, he had spoken. I took Karen from school that evening and I laid my hand on her stomach and pleaded the blood of Jesus: "the blood of Jesus, the blood of Jesus, the blood of Jesus". I pleaded the blood of Jesus for what must have been the best part of an hour. She went to the toilet and shouted, "Mummy, my stomach ache has gone". She was very excited, praise the Lord. Jesus is the truth.

The Lord then said to me, "I have given you the blood". I have taken it and I use it for everything. There is power in the blood of Jesus. Before that day I knew very little about the power over the devil's work when the blood of Jesus is appropriated. I knew that Jesus had shed his blood to take away the sins of the human race, but I did not know much more about the precious blood of Jesus. The church I went to was a small Pentecostal church where we learned only the basics of Christianity. On this particular day God revealed the importance of the blood of Jesus in our Christian walk.

For a whole week after that miraculous day, I woke up at about 5.00 am and read all the Psalms of thanksgiving and praise. I praised God for hours and gave him thanks for his love and for the power of his blood. I thought of how I would have been organizing my son's funeral and

I gave Jesus all the thanks in the universe. The Psalms helped me to praise the Lord because I could not find words to adore and thank and praise the Lord enough.

I received a revelation of the blood of Jesus on that day of miracles and I have gone on to learn more as the Lord opens up my understanding and reveals scripture on the blood of Jesus. I have done studies on the blood of Jesus and continue to do so. The Lord is using the ministry on the blood of Jesus to scatter demons, heal bodies, clean up homes, etc. Plead the blood of Jesus. The devil and his demons do not like when the church sounds out the blood of Jesus, it cripples them.

The revelation Jesus gave me of the power of his blood came through a very hard experience, but it was well worth it. The life of the flesh is in the blood and as I pleaded the blood of Jesus it gave life to my son.

As I share what the Lord has revealed to me on the blood of Jesus and what he is revealing, I trust all who read this book will get all their needs met as they learn to plead the blood of Jesus.

CHAPTER 2

THE LIFE OF THE FLESH IS IN THE BLOOD

St John 6:47-56

St John 6:47-56 47. Verily, verily I say unto you, He that believeth on me hath everlasting life. 48. I am that bread of life. 49. Your fathers did eat manna in the wilderness and are dead. 50. This is the bread which cometh down from heaven, that a man may eat thereof, and not die. 51. I am the living bread which came down from heaven: if any man eat of this bread, he shall live forever: and the bread that I will give is my flesh, which I will give for the life of the world. 52. The Jews therefore strove among themselves, saying, How can this man give us his flesh to eat? 53. Then Jesus said unto them, Verily, verily, I say unto you, Except ye eat the flesh of the Son of man, and drink his blood, ye have no life in you. 54. Whoso eateth my flesh, and drinketh my blood, hath eternal life, and I will raise him up at the last day. 55. For my flesh is meat indeed and my blood is drink indeed. 56. He that eateth my flesh, and drinketh my blood, dwelleth in me, and I in him. Genesis 2:7 And the Lord God formed man of the dust of the ground, and breathed into his nostrils the breath of life; and man became a living soul.

As I ministered on the radio one Sunday morning on "The blood of Jesus", the Lord opened my eyes to the fact that his breath activated, miraculously, the flow of blood into the human body to cause him to become alive. Without the flow of blood in man's body he would not become alive because the life of the flesh is in the blood. Leviticus 17:11 For the life of the flesh is in the blood: and I have given it to you upon the altar to make an atonement for your souls: for it is the blood that maketh an atonement for the soul.

The life of God was poured into man. However, when man sinned the blood dried out of him and the life of God left him. He died. Ezekiel 18:4 Behold, all souls are mine; as the soul of the father, so also the soul of the son is mine: the soul that sinneth, it shall die. Satan told the woman: Ye shall not surely die. [Genesis 3:4]. However, the word of God is the truth, the whole human race died physically and spiritually because man sinned.

The people of God ate manna in the wilderness. The Lord caused this bread to fall from heaven. Exodus 16:14-15 14. And when the dew that lay was gone up, behold upon the face of the wilderness there lay a small round thing, as small as the hoar frost on the ground. 15. And when the children of Israel saw it, they said one to another, it is manna: for they wist not what it was. And Moses said unto them, This is the bread which the Lord hath given you to eat.

Jesus came down from heaven, representing the true bread. The manna was the shadow bread. The Israelites ate the shadow bread and died. Jesus said that all who believed and ate of him shall live. Jesus is the living bread that gives everlasting life.

When Jesus told the Jews that man needed to eat this true and living bread, they became confused as are many today who try to work out the ways of God. His ways are past finding out. The confusion of the religious leaders increased when Jesus went on to explain that "except ye eat the flesh of the Son of man and drink his blood, ye have no life in you" [St John 6:53].

The life giving blood of God that dried up when man sinned would be replaced in man and would raise him up from death unto life if he would believe.

The love of God would not allow man to remain dead and that is why Jesus came down from heaven and shed his blood and made it available to believers so that they could drink of it and live. The blood that Jesus shed would replace the blood that had dried out of man when he sinned and died.

Today, all man needs to do is to have faith in what Jesus accomplished at the cross of Calvary when he said "It is finished". St John 19:30: When Jesus therefore had received the vinegar, he said, It is finished: and he bowed his head and gave up the ghost.

Most of us know that someone can bleed to death. If someone has had an accident, or something happens that is causing too much bleeding, the doctors are quick to give a blood transfusion because if the blood leaves the body there will be no life. This is a spiritual matter. Therefore, lost blood must quickly be replaced or one gets very weak. The blood is man's life and strength.

Satan and his demons must have had trembling knees when it struck true to them what Jesus had done on that cross when he shed his blood. The people who died, through rebellion against God, with the full assistance of the devil, were becoming alive again, by the blood of Jesus, and would be overthrowing the devil's kingdom. Under the Old Testament, the use of blood to make atonement was most important.

What is the meaning of atonement?

The dictionary definition - **Atone**: Compensate for, make amends for, pay the penalty for, recompense for, pay the price for.

Leviticus 17:11.......for it is the blood that maketh atonement for the soul. It is right then to understand that it is the blood that pays the price for the soul.

Under the Old Covenant, the high priest had to make atonement for the altar, the holy place, the tabernacle of the congregation, all the vessels of the sanctuary and the people. Most importantly, he must sprinkle the mercy seat with blood. However, before he could make atonement for anyone, he first had to atone for himself and his household. We must cover ourselves and our household with the blood of Jesus.

The high priest sprinkled the blood for cleansing. Leviticus 16:14-15 14. And he [Aaron, the high priest] shall take of the blood of the bullock and sprinkle it with his finger upon the mercy seat eastward and before the mercy seat shall he sprinkle of the blood with his finger seven times. 15. Then shall he kill the goat of the sin offering, that is for the people and bring his blood within the veil, and do with that blood as he did with the blood of the bullock, and sprinkle it upon the mercy seat, and before the mercy seat.

Leviticus 16:18-19, 30 18. And he shall go out unto the altar that is before the Lord and make an atonement for it, and shall take of the blood of the bullock and of the blood of the goat, and put it upon the horns of the altar round about. 19. And he shall sprinkle of the blood upon it with his finger seven times and cleanse it, and hallow it from the uncleanness of the children of Israel. 30. For on that day shall the priest make an atonement for you to cleanse you, that ye may be clean from all your sins before the Lord.

Here, the sprinkled blood was cleansing the people and covering their sins. It was on the outside. They were not commanded to drink the blood. On the contary they were not to eat blood. Drinking of blood was to wait for the Lord Jesus Christ. The blood that the high priest sprinkled did not give spiritual life. It did not minister a change of heart. The same act had to be performed every year. The blood of Jesus, however, was shed once. All we have to do is to apply it by faith, praise the Lord.

Hebrews 9:25-28 25. Nor yet that he should offer himself often, as the high priest entereth into the holy place every year with blood of others. 26. For then must he often have suffered since the foundation of the world: but now once in the end of the world hath he appeared to put away sin by the sacrifice of himself. 25. And as it is appointed unto men once to die, but after this the judgement: 28. So Christ was once offered to bear the sins of many: and unto them that look for him shall he appear the second time without sin unto salvation.

The blood of Jesus has been shed. The price has been paid. We have been redeemed. We do not have to wait for a day of atonement to sprinkle the blood. It is available to us as often as we need it. Sprinkle the blood. Satan and his demons know about Jesus' blood; plead it and drive the demons away. I plead the blood of Jesus for everything and I teach this to the people. The sound of the blood of Jesus cripples satan and his servants.

Mother W received the revelation of the blood of Jesus after she received her healing in church and she went home to practise the use of the blood of Jesus. She pleaded the blood of Jesus, by faith, on her unsaved husband's hurting foot. It worked. God delivered him. She then walked about the house saying "the blood of Jesus, the blood of Jesus, the blood of Jesus". Mr W's mind was not made up to serve the Lord and the pleading of the blood of Jesus tormented him. "This blood of Jesus" shouted Mr W and through the door he went. The blood of Jesus is powerful to deliver and bless the people of God, but it can bring destruction to the Lord's enemies. Get on the Lord's side and plead the blood of Jesus.

Mother W bought one of our cassette tapes on the ministry of the blood of Jesus. She put this tape to play in her home. To her amazement the songs that went along with the teaching on the blood of Jesus had Mr W dancing around the house. The voice of the blood of Jesus drove out the demons of unbelief and freed up Mr W to take his wife and a couple of sisters in his car to church. Needless to say Mother W is continuing to play the tapes in her home.

Mr W has asked Mother W where have all her diseases gone. Mr W has noticed that Mother W is no longer ill. The Lord has healed all mother W's illnesses. Mr W has also noticed how strong she has become and would like to know how this has come about! Mother W has told her husband that she has learned to plead the blood of Jesus. Plead the blood of Jesus over all of your situations and circumstances and receive the victory. Good success is yours in Jesus' name.

My testimony by Evangelist RF

Jesus saves: St Luke 19:10 For the Son of man is come to seek and to save that which was lost.

Jesus is wonderful. Satan had set out to destroy me from a child but God had plans for my life and he kept me alive.

The story goes that whilst I was but a toddler I died, but Jesus raised me from the dead. As time went on and I and my siblings grew, my parents emigrated to the UK and we were left with relatives. There was plenty of play space as we lived in the countryside and we all played and had fun; we were happy. However, the time came for us to leave the Caribbean and join our parents in the UK.

Things were different in the new country. Days were often cold as we went to school and playing out was not the same as playing out in the open fields back home. As children, we got used to things, got our education and found work. Some of the older ones got married and left home.

Satan had plans for my life, however, and when my behaviour became unsatisfactory [possibly, due to the change] I was put out of the family home at the tender age of 16 years. I found it hard going living away from home and satan provided me with people with whom I could gamble to try and raise money to help me with my financial problems. I found part-time jobs whilst I went to college to educate myself but the demon of gambling had moved in on me.

At the age of just over 20 years I found a lovely girl and got married. She was vaguely aware that I gambled, but I am confident she did not understand the seriousness of having a gambler as a husband. I am sure I did not realize how evil gambling was at the time. We were both quite young.

We started to have a family and we were both working. We worked very hard and I continued to study. I enjoyed studying but I had what I discovered to be "an evil disease"; I was hooked on gambling. I earned very good money. Large sums of money for my hard work only passed through my hands. Not only did I have a good job which paid a high salary, I did lots of private jobs in the evenings and at weekends for which I earned large sums of money.

The demon of gambling was having a field day in my life. The larger the sums of money I earned the bigger the bet I would place on the horses and the more the money I would take to the gambling casinos. I was a highly qualified engineer and very highly qualified electrician. I wired whole houses for large sums of money. My work was very professional and I was never short of jobs. Work was never scarce as my fame spread far and wide and there were more jobs for me than I could handle.

The evil spirit of gambling watched me carefully and bound me up so tightly that I began to gamble monies people gave me to buy material for their jobs. Obviously, I could not do the jobs because I had lost the people's monies at the gambling table. I gambled thousands of pounds at times. Nearly all my earnings went on gambling.

Christians I knew, and there were many of them, did all they could to help me find a relationship with the Lord. I wanted to be saved but I found it especially hard. I would give my heart to the Lord, get baptized and attend church for a while. However, I would hear of a horse that was running which sounded a winner and my heart would yearn to recover at least some of the large sums of money I had lost [in the devil's kingdom you can only lose] and I would fall back into the pit hole of gambling. I felt helpless at times and I began to lie as I lost people's monies at the gambling casinos and could not finish off their jobs. I had to find all kinds of excuses to explain away why jobs were incomplete. I sometimes hid from people as I tried hard to win some money to straighten things out. This meant borrowing more monies to gamble and getting myself into more problems. The spiders' webs got more and more entangled. My wages would go into the bank. I would gamble all of it because I needed a big win to clear off all my debts. I would lose all of it and had a month to go without money. There was obviously no monies going into my home. My wife was left to pay all the bills and take care of the family. There were six children born to the marriage.

Things got worse as the days went by. Monies I had borrowed to gamble needed to be paid back, my family was suffering, my wife was very unhappy. My life was a mess. People were searching for me in anger to recover their monies and others were demanding that their jobs be completed. I became very hard hearted and deceitful. I had to be that way, to stay sane. I loved my beautiful wife and my lovely children who loved me, and I realized that it was God alone who could help me. I was in trouble. I began to lie to the people I loved so much: my wife and my children. I made promises to them which I was never able to keep. I was a prisoner to gambling. On a Friday evening when my wife would be waiting for me to bring in the housekeeping money I would just disappear. Worse than that, I would somehow manage to get hold of any money she had and was not careful to hide, and I would gamble that as well. I made her life, and the lives of my children, hell. Things got so bad the children did not believe anything I told them. [They had a right not to believe anything I said, because I was never able to keep promises I had made them].

There was often no food in our house and no money to pay the bills. My wife would try and pay what she could, [if I did not get hold of her money], and she bought the food. I would try really hard and for a few weeks I would bring in some money into the home and things would start to look up. Satan would disagree with this completely and I would just fall down again and make my family very unhappy.

My mother-in-law, Apostle Lake, prayed for me day and night. She tried all she could to settle me in Christ. I wanted to serve the Lord but it was hard. No one could help me but Jesus. I would be in and out of the church; eventually I just gave up and stopped going. My wife, a dedicated Christian would continue to go and take the children. I became hardened and so my wife stopped inviting me. My mother-in-law decided that only prayer could help and she prayed. My wife prayed. Prayer works, Jesus hears and answers prayers. I had made a promise to my mother-in-law that I would help her with the ministry work and although I was not saved the Lord would have me to remember my promise, praise the Lord.

I was at work one day and the Lord visited me on the job with these words: "When did you last go to church?". I thought about it and asked myself the question: "When did I last go to church?" That was my turning point. No one else could do it. These seemingly simple words were powerful from the mouth of the Lord. I made it up in my mind there and then that I would go to church and that I would serve the Lord.

Isaiah 49:24-25 24. Shall the prey be taken from the mighty, or the lawful captive delivered? 25. But thus saith the Lord, Even the captives of the mighty shall be taken away, and the prey of the terrible shall be delivered: for I will contend with them that contendeth with thee and I will save thy children.

I was a prey to satan and a captive to his devices, but Jesus delivered me. I went to church and have continued to go. I work for the Lord with all my heart. I am an ordained evangelist and I stand alongside Apostle Lake in the ministry. I drive up and down and take her to the meetings and I am happy doing this. I feel good because I am now able to keep my promise to help her with the work of the Lord. And my family? My wife has never been happier and my children have never been happier. I now have time to instruct them in the ways of the Lord. The change in my life is remarkable. I take care of my home financially. I am now closer than ever to my children. No one is looking for me for their money and I have no unfinished jobs, and since the Lord delivered me he has healed a very painful leg which I had.

To the Lord Jesus Christ be all the praise, honour and glory. Thank you Jesus for delivering me!

Whatever your condition, God can solve it. Do not give up. There is light at the end of the tunnel.

CHAPTER 3

GOD CLOTHED THE FIRST COUPLE WITH ANIMAL SKIN

Genesis 3:1-15 1. Now the serpent was more subtil than any beast of the field which the Lord God had made. And he said unto the woman, Yea, hath God said ye shall not eat of every tree of the garden? 2. And the woman said unto the serpent, We may eat of the fruit of the trees of the garden: 3. But of the fruit of the tree which is in the midst of the garden, God hath said, Ye shall not eat of it, neither shall ye touch it, lest ye die. 4. And the serpent said unto the woman, Ye shall not surely die; 5. For God doth know that in the day ye eat thereof, then your eyes shall be opened and ye shall be as gods, knowing good and evil. 6. And when the woman saw that the tree was good for food, and that it was pleasant to the eyes and a tree to be desired to make one wise, she took of the fruit thereof, and did eat, and gave also unto her husband with her, and he did eat. 7.And the eyes of them both were opened and they knew that they were naked and they sewed fig leaves together and made themselves aprons. 8. And they heard the voice of the Lord God walking in the garden in the cool of the day: and Adam and his wife hid themselves from the presence of the Lord God amongst the trees of the garden. 9. And the Lord God called unto Adam, and said unto him, Where art thou? 10. And he said, I heard thy voice in the garden, and I was afraid, because I was naked: and I hid myself. 11. And he said, Who told thee that thou wast naked? Hast Thou eaten of the tree, whereof I commanded thee that thou shouldest not eat? 12. And the man said, The woman whom thou gavest to be with me, she gave me of the tree, and I did eat. 13. And the Lord God said unto the woman, What is this that thou hast done? And the woman said, The serpent beguiled me, and I did eat. 14. And the Lord God said unto the serpent, Because thou hast done this, thou art cursed above all cattle, and above every beast of the field; upon thy belly shalt thou go, and dust shalt thou eat all the days of thy life. 15. And I will put enmity between thee and the woman, and between thy seed and her seed, it shall bruise thy head, and thou shalt bruise his heel.

Satan deceived the couple and caused the life of God to depart from them. I believe that as they ate the forbidden fruit the life of God left them. Every time they chewed that fruit the life blood ebbed away so that by the time they had finished eating they were dead.Satan grabbed hold of all the authority, love, health and strength, wisdom, anointing and power that God had given to the man.

They sold themselves to the devil and the package they received had "hell" written on it. As they opened this, every wind of fear, disease germs, hate and bitterness, witchcraft, idolatry, fornication, murder and weakness blew into their faces. They saw themselves naked and they were ashamed, so ashamed that they sewed fig leaves and made aprons to cover their nakedness. Fig leaves could not cover their shame. It was their life blood that had been lost and needed to be replaced by the mercies of God.

In verse 8 the voice of the Lord sounded out, and they fled. What a state they found themselves in! a great fall from having fellowship with God to being afraid of God. It was God's holiness that had them running. The Lord was obviously sad and disappointed as they hid themselves from him. Adam, where are you? God called the man. He was given responsibility which he had neglected. We need to be very careful that we do not allow even the closest person to us to divert us from the call of God upon our lives. We are answerable to God.

Genesis 3:10-11 10. I heard your voice in the garden and I was afraid because I was naked and I hid myself. 11. Who told you that you were naked, have you eaten of the tree I commanded you not to eat? People who do not know the Lord are always afraid of his voice. Sin brings separation from God.

Instead of repenting, Adam began to make excuses by almost blaming God for giving him a disobedient wife. We must face up to our wrongs. Adam had a mind of his own to make decisions. He made the wrong decision and should have faced up to it. The word says, So then everyone of us shall give account of himself to God [Romans 14:12]. What is this thou hast done? said the Lord God unto the woman. Another poorly excuse was heard: The serpent beguiled me, she replied [Genesis 3:13].

There is something of note here. God asked the man a question: Where are you? He also asked the woman a question: What is this that thou hast done? God did not, however, ask the serpent a question. He directed a straight curse at that evil being. Because thou hast done this, thou art cursed above all cattle, and above every beast of the field; upon thy belly shalt thou go, and dust shalt thou eat all the days of thy life. And I will put enmity between thee and the woman and between thy seed and her seed: it shall bruise thy head and thou shalt bruise his heel [Genesis 3:14-15]. Why did not God ask the serpent a question? The Lord was dealing directly with satan. He was making the devil know that despite what he had done, there were plans for his demise and his judgement was already settled.

The devil, of course, did not quite understand what God would do. If he did, he would have allowed Pilate and the religious leaders to release Jesus. He would never have allowed Jesus' blood to be shed. He would have gone easy on things and Jesus would not have received the stripes by which we are healed. St John 19:34 But one of the soldiers with a spear pierced his side and forthwith came there out blood and water". Isaiah 53:5 But he was wounded for our transgressions, he was bruised for our iniquities; the chastisement of our peace was upon him; and with his stripes we are healed.

Disobedience and rebellion against God's word is punishable and brings the curse. The man was cursed by the Lord with hard work to survive. He would have to sweat it out. In fact, even the earth was cursed because of his sin. The earth would help to make his life hard. The word of God stands fast for ever.

Genesis 2:17 But of the tree of the knowledge of good and evil, thou shalt not eat of it, for in the day that thou eatest thereof thou shalt surely die. Man was to have a slow death. He would live a life of sickness, sorrow and suffering until he physically died. Because the Lord's blood had dried out of him when he sinned, he had already died spiritually.

Unto the woman the curse was of suffering and sorrow during childbirth. Genesis 3:16 I will greatly multiply thy sorrow and thy conception; in sorrow thou shalt bring forth children; and thy desire shalt be to thy husband, and he shall rule over thee.

God had told the couple to multiply and replenish the earth. Because they disobeyed the word of God the woman was to suffer during childbirth. She was to be the man's helper but because of their sin he would rule over her. However, God's love for man was so powerful that it made the way for God to cover man's sin in order that he may continue to have fellowship with him.

Genesis 3:21 And unto Adam also and to his wife did the Lord God make coats of skins and clothed them.

It was not God's desire that man should sin but the Lord knew that having given them freedom of choice they would fall under the wiles of the devil and disobey him. In their disobedience they handed over to the devil the authority God had given them over his creation. In doing this, they took the whole human race with them down the streets of rebellion towards God.

The love of God is greater far than tongue or pen can ever tell. God made man, a beautiful creature, to share fellowship with him and God would see that it remained that way, despite the deception of the devil. Satan and his demons must have gloated at the condition of man, but God had a plan for man's redemption.

When Jesus breathed in man the breath of life, blood flowed through man's body and man became a living soul. There is no life without blood. However, when man sinned, as previously stated, the blood of God disappeared and man died, not only physically but also spiritually. Blood would need to be put back into man to bring him back to life.

In the garden of Eden, God walked past the devil and sacrificed an animal in order to release blood to cover man's sins. Man was given his first fur coat lined with blood. It was not the skin that covered man's sin it was the blood underneath the skin. It was the blood that made the atonement for the couple's souls. Satan had lost; God had rescued man. The way was made for man's relationship to be restored with God. The shadow was in place, waiting for the reality. This was the start of an innumerable amount of animal sacrifices, until Christ came.

2 Chronicles 7:5 And king Solomon offered a sacrifice of twenty and two thousand oxen, and an hundred and twenty thousand sheep, so the king and all the people dedicated the house of God. This was a dedication service and required a lot of blood to purify and bless the place. In our dedication services we purify and bless the place by pleading the blood of Jesus; it works.

When we have moved into a new building to be used for the Lord's work we have pleaded the blood of Jesus, and have sprinkled it by faith and poured it out throughout the building. From my experience, when we have done this, the Holy Ghost fire has fallen upon the service and signs and wonders have taken place. Pour out and sprinkle the blood of Jesus. Victory is guaranteed in Jesus' name.

My testimony by M W

Praises be to the Lord Jesus.

I became pregnant and went to the doctor who sent me to the local hospital. They did the usual tests for pregnant women. They discovered I was HIV positive. You can imagine how shocked I was. I had another partner previously and I was not sure who gave me this disease.

I heard Apostle Lake broadcasting on the radio on a Sunday morning. She seemed to minister with fire. I was drawn to the way she prayed and decided to ring the given number for prayer. I knew that only God could help me. The doctors were not able to help me and I cried. At the time I rang, Apostle Lake was very busy and asked me to ring later. I did. She was again pressed for time as she was rushing off to a meeting for which she was already late. She asked for my number and offered to ring me as soon as she was able. I burst into tears, as I was desperate. "Please, I have to go to the hospital tomorrow for tests, give me even a little prayer." She gave in and prayed for me. The next day I went to the hospital and they took lots of blood and did various tests. They did these very often, partly because I was expecting a baby. They were treating the baby in the womb and keeping a close watch on it to stop the baby being born with this evil disease.

After Apostle Lake had prayed for me, she gave me the venues and times of their meetings. The Thursday evening prayer house of fire was near to where I lived and I settled it in my heart that I would attend this. I went to the prayer house on the Thursday evening. I felt very comfortable and confident that the Lord would help me. The time came for those who needed prayer to go forward. I was one of the first ones to go forward. The congregation pleaded the blood of Jesus very loudly. In fact, nearly all the prayers seemed to have started with "the blood of Jesus".

Apostle Lake brought me to salvation in the Lord Jesus. I accepted Jesus Christ as my personal saviour and Apostle Lake took authority over the disease germs. She bound and drove them out and commanded them to die by fire. The power of the Holy Ghost blew me onto the floor. Jesus dealt with me. I began to attend all the Thursday evening meetings and also the Sabbath services at the same venue. A month went by and I went for my usual tests at the hospital. I also had further tests at my General Practitioner's surgery. They promised to send the results to me in the normal way. Previously, the tests were positive. This time, however, the hospital rang me. The tests were negative. There was no trace of any HIV whatsoever. I was healed. They asked me what had happened. I told them I had gone for prayer and the Lord had healed me. I now attend Apostle Lake's ministry where I am witnessing miracles, signs and wonders. They certainly do plead the blood of Jesus at this ministry.

Whenever things do not seem to be going right, I plead the blood of Jesus and the Lord performs miracles for me.

Plead the blood of Jesus when you have problems, victory is sure.

CHAPTER 4

CUTTING THE COVENANT WITH BLOOD

Genesis 15:5-14 5. And he brought him forth abroad and said, Look now toward heaven, and tell the stars if thou be able to number them: and he said unto him, So shall thy seed be. 6. And he believed in the Lord and he counted it to him for righteousness. 7. And he said unto him, I am the Lord that brought thee out of Ur of the Chaldees, to give thee this land to inherit it. 8. And he said, Lord God, whereby shall I know that I shall inherit it? 9. And he said unto him, Take me an heifer of three years old, and a she goat of three years old and a ram of three years old, and a turtle dove, and a young pigeon. 10. And he took unto him all these and divided them in the midst, and laid each piece one against another: but the birds divided he not. 11. And when the fowls came down upon the carcases, Abram drove them away. 12. And when the sun was going down, a deep sleep fell upon Abram; and lo, an horror of great darkness fell upon him. 13. And he said unto Abram, know of a surety that thy seed shall be a stranger in a land that is not theirs, and shall serve them; and they shall afflict them four hundred years: 14. And also that nation whom they shall serve, will I judge: and afterward shall they come out with great substance.

Our God is a covenant making and a covenant keeping God. God made a promise to Abram, that he would multiply him as the stars of heaven. Abram believed

God and he was accounted righteous before the Lord. The covenant made with Abram was not without blood. God himself initiated animal sacrifices at the very time he slew the animal to cover the sins of Adam and Eve.

God told Abram to get some three year old animals and a couple of birds. He was to cut the animals in two and place them one against another. He should not divide the birds. The carcases were laid out but some fowls came down upon these. Abram drove them away. There will always be fowls who will want to come down upon your sacrifices. Drive them away. Their intention is to eat up your blessings. Abram's sacrifice was for him to receive God's covenant blessings. Some fowls don't like when we are making our covenant sacrifice of blessings. These demons would like to eat up our sacrifices and hinder the blessings upon us and our descendants.

Dismiss those evil speakers and send those demons flying by fire. By the time they reach the pit they would have been nearly burnt out.

When our blood sacrifice goes up the Lord's power comes down. After Abram's sacrifice a deep sleep fell upon him and he received the prophecy of what would happen to his decendants. Obviously, the Lord did not go into this in detail at that time but the word gives the details: Exodus 12:12-13 12. For I will pass through the land of Egypt this night and will smite all the firstborn in the land of Egypt, both man and beast, and against all the gods of Egypt I will execute judgement, I am the Lord. And the blood shall be to you for a token upon the houses where ye are, and when I see the blood I will pass over you, and the plague shall not be upon you to destroy you, when I smite the land of Egypt. The covenant God made with Abram was a blood covenant which God has kept.

As we search the scriptures we see that God works with blood. There is life in the blood.

Genesis 17:11-14 11. And ye shall circumcise the flesh of your foreskin, and it shall be a token of the covenant betwixt me and you. 12. And he that is eight days old shall be circumcised among you, every man child in your generation, he that is born in the house, or bought with money of any stranger, which is not of thy seed. 13. He that is born in the house, and he that is bought with thy money, must needs be circumcised, and my covenant shall be in your flesh for an everlasting covenant. 14. And the uncircumcised man child whose flesh of his foreskin is not circumcised, that soul shall be cut off from his people, he hath broken my covenant.

God had made a covenant with Abraham. His name had now been changed. Abraham means "the father of many nations". Genesis 17:4-5 4. As for me, behold my covenant is with thee, and thou shalt be a father of many nations. 5. Neither shall thy name any more be called Abram, but thy name shall be Abraham, for a father of many nations have I made thee.

The covenant was in Abraham's flesh of his foreskin [the reproductive part of his body]. Blood had to be shed here, since the life of the flesh is in the blood, and the blood would seal the covenant. Genesis 17:11 And he shall circumcise the flesh of your foreskin and it shall be a token of the covenant betwixt me and you.

When Abraham's descendants were coming out of Egyptian bondage as God had promised, the blood was also a token upon the houses . Exodus 12:13 And the blood shall be to you for a token upon the houses where ye are, and when I see the blood I will pass over you, and the plague shall not be upon you to destroy you, when I smite the land of Egypt.

Under the Old Covenant, the Lord used the blood of animals to seal covenants and houses; today he uses the precious blood of Jesus. We are very blessed. We don't need to slay animals to get basins of blood. All we need to do is to apply the blood of Jesus by speaking it like this: "the blood of Jesus over this house, the blood of Jesus upon my children, the blood of Jesus upon my job". It has been made so easy for us by the Lord Jesus Christ. May Jesus be for ever glorified

The covenant of circumcision included Abraham's children and anyone else in his home who belonged to him, for example, his servants or slaves whom he had bought. This blood circumcision included his household. Genesis 17:13 He that is born in thy house, and he that is bought with thy money, must needs be circumcised, and my covenant shall be in your flesh for an everlasting covenant.

That blood covenant included all who belonged to Abraham. Paul and Silas were delivered from prison in Philippi and in the middle of the night as they worked at bringing the Philippian jailor to an experience with Christ they said, as recorded in Acts 16:31 Believe on the Lord Jesus Christ and thou shalt be saved and thy house. The blood of Jesus brings salvation to the whole family, praise the Lord. Bring your family under the blood of Jesus Christ.

Deuteronomy 10:16-17 16.Circumcise, therefore, the foreskin of your heart, and be no more stiff-necked. 17. For the Lord your God is God of gods, and Lord of lords, a great God, a mighty and a terrible, which regardeth not persons, nor taketh reward.

Moses admonished the Israelites to cut the hard parts of their hearts away and put away their stiff-neckedness. Today, the blood of Jesus will remove every hard covering from our hearts so that the Lord may enter in his fulness. It is no more a circumcision of the flesh, it is a circumcision of the heart. Romans 2:29 But he is a Jew, which is one inwardly; and circumcision is that of the heart, in the spirit, and not in the letter, whose praise is not of men but of God.

For those of us who know the Lord as God of gods and Lord of lords, a great God, a mighty and terrible God, the blood of Jesus Christ is available for us to use and be blessed. The blood is our seal and covering. Seal and cover your homes and families with it by faith. God will honour this. How do I do it? Simply plead the blood of Jesus over them: "the blood of Jesus over my home, the blood of Jesus over my family". You should confess this until you feel released in your spirit that it is realized in the spirit realm, you will know when it is. Walk by faith and praise the Lord.

Jeremiah 4:4 Circumcise yourselves to the Lord and take away the foreskins of your heart…

Colossians 2:11 In whom also ye are circumcised with the circumcision made without hands in putting off the body of the sins of the flesh by the circumcision of Christ.

CHAPTER 5

GOD TESTED ABRAHAM [A SHADOW OF CHRIST]

Genesis:18:9-14 9. And they said unto him, Where is Sarah thy wife? And he said, Behold, in the tent. 10. And he said, I will certainly return unto thee according to the time of life; and lo, Sarah thy wife shall have a son, And Sarah heard it in the tent door, which was behind him. 11. Now Abraham and Sarah were old and well stricken in age; and it ceased to be with Sarah after the manner of women. 12. Therefore Sarah laughed within herself, saying, After I am waxed old shall I have pleasure, my lord being old also? 13. And the Lord said unto Abraham, Wherefore did Sarah laugh, saying, Shall I of a surety bear a child, which am old? 14. Is anything too hard for the Lord? At the time appointed I will return unto thee, according to the time of life, and Sarah shall have a son.

The Lord appeared to Abraham and promised that Sarah would have a child. Sarah laughed because she was past child-bearing age and Abraham was an old man. The Lord visited Sarah as he had said and the Lord did unto Sarah as he had spoken. She conceived and bore Abraham a son in his old age at the set time the Lord had said. Abraham named his son Isaac and Abraham circumcised his son when he was eight days old. Blood had to flow. The promised blessing must remain by way of the covenant of circumcision. God is a covenant keeping God and we must keep our part of the covenant.

The blood from the circumcision was very important in the eyes of the Lord.

Genesis 21:1-4 1. And the Lord visited Sarah as he had said, and the Lord did unto Sarah as he had spoken. 2. For Sarah conceived, and bare Abraham a son in his old age, at the set time of which God had spoken to him. 3. And Abraham called the name of his son that was born unto him, whom Sarah bare to him, Isaac. 4. And Abraham circumcised his son Isaac being eight days old, as God had commanded him.

The time had come for Abraham to be put to the test. This would be quite a severe test that would require complete faith in God. The Lord had told Abraham that the heir of the promise would be Isaac. Genesis 21:10, 12 10. Wherefore she said unto Abraham, Cast out this bondwoman and her son: for the son of this bondwoman shall not be heir with my son, even with Isaac. 12. And God said unto Abraham, Let it not be grievous in thy sight because of the lad, and because of thy bondwoman; in all that Sarah hath said unto thee, hearken unto her voice; for in Isaac shall thy seed be called. Genesis 22:1-19 1. And it came to pass after these things that God did tempt Abraham, and said unto him, Abraham: and he said, Behold, here am I. 2. And he said, take now thy son, thine only son Isaac, whom thou lovest, and get thee into the land of Moriah; and offer him there for a burnt offering upon one of the mountains which I will tell thee of. 3. And Abraham rose up early in the morning, and saddled his ass, and took two of his young men with him, and Isaac his son and clave the wood for the burnt offering, and rose up and went unto the place of which God had told him. 4. Then on the third day Abraham lifted up his eyes, and saw the place afar off. 5. And

Abraham said unto his young men, Abide ye here with the ass; and I and the lad will go yonder and worship, and come again to you. 6. And Abraham took the wood of the burnt offering, and laid it upon Isaac his son, and he took the fire in his hand, and a knife; and they went both of them together. 7. And Isaac spake unto Abraham his father, and said, My father: and he said, Here am I, my son. And he said, Behold the fire and the wood: but where is the lamb for a burnt offering? 8. And Abraham said, My son, God will provide himself a lamb for a burnt offering: so they went both of them together. 9. And they came to the place which God had told him of: and Abraham built an altar there, and laid the wood in order, and bound Isaac his son, and laid him on the altar upon the wood. 10. And Abraham stretched forth his hand, and took the knife to slay his son. 11. And the angel of the Lord called to him out of heaven, and said, Abraham, Abraham: and he said, Here am I. 12. And he said, Lay not thine hand upon the lad, neither do thou anything unto him; for now I know that thou fearest God, seeing thou hast not withheld thy son, thine only son from me. 13. And Abraham lifted up his eyes, and looked, and behold behind him a ram caught in a thicket by his horns; and Abraham went and took the ram, and offered him up for a burnt offering in the stead of his son. 14. And Abraham called the name of that place Jehovah-jireh: as it is said to this day. In the mount of the Lord it shall be seen. 15. And the angel of the Lord called unto Abraham out of heaven the second time, 16. And said, By myself have I sworn, saith the Lord, for because thou hast done this thing and hast not withheld thy son, thine only son: 17. That in blessing I will bless thee, and in multiplying I will multiply thy seed as the stars of the heaven, and as the sand which is upon the sea shore; and thy seed shall possess the gate of his enemies.

18. And in thy seed shall all the nations of the earth be blessed: because thou hast obeyed my voice. 19. So Abraham returned unto his young men, and they rose up and went together to Beersheba; and Abraham dwelt at Beersheba.

Abraham was commanded by the Lord to offer up as a sacrifice the heir of the promise, whom he loved and through whom the promise would be fulfilled. Abraham would be a type of Christ, offering up a blood sacrifice in obedience to the word of God, and also a type of the Father who would give up as a sacrifice his only son.

Abraham was totally committed to God and did not ponder over what the Lord had asked him to do. He rose up early in the morning and saddled his donkey, took two of his young men and Isaac his son and took the wood for the burnt offering and travelled towards the place of which the Lord had told him. What faith!!

They travelled for three days and the place of which the Lord had told Abraham was in view. Can you see the place where the Lord is leading you, your place of sacrifice where you will receive your covenant blessing? Is it in view? Keep going. You cannot take others with you. God is dealing with you. Genesis 22:5 And Abraham said unto his young men, Abide ye here with the ass, and I and the lad will go yonder and worship, and come again. We come to the place where we must meet with God alone, others might distract or discourage us.

I shudder to think how I would feel as I laid the wood on my only son and took the fire and the knife in my hand. This reminds me of our heavenly Father as he looked at his one and only son with the burden of the whole world upon him, knowing that the spear [knife] would be pierced in his side. The sacrifice was staring Abraham in the face as it did Jesus, who was to sacrifice himself. In obedience to the Father he must go on to that mountain. It is not surprising that Isaac asked his father where was the lamb for the burnt offering, since that was missing. Genesis 22:8 .....My son, God will provide himself a lamb for a burnt offering.... This was Abraham's reply. Abraham truly believed that God could raise up Isaac. Make that sacrifice, God will provide.

It takes a certain type of person to make this type of sacrifice, he has to be totally committed to the Father's will. Luke 22:41-42 41 And he was withdrawn from them about a stone's cast, and kneeled down and prayed, Saying, Father if thou be willing remove this cup from me; nevertheless, not my will but thine be done.. Verses 9-10 of Genesis 22 are of special note.

Abraham and his son Isaac had reached the place of their sacrificial offering. Isaac went along with his father willingly and his father was offering him up willingly. The altar was built, the wood was laid in order and Isaac was bound and laid upon the altar. A sacrifice indeed! What a wonderful type of God giving his Son.

Jesus was placed on a cross of wood to die. Note: Isaac was laid on the wood. Abraham in giving up Isaac believed that God was able to raise him up again. When Jesus went on the cross, he knew he would be raised from death triumphantly. [1 Corinthians 15:21 For since by man came death, by man came also the resurrection of the dead]. Abraham stretched forth his hand to slay the lad. Abraham's complete faith in God moved God's heart and the Lord provided, in accordance with

Abraham's faith, a ram for the sacrifice. A blood sacrifice was necessary, since Abraham would be the father of many nations and the life of the flesh is in the blood.

Abraham's love for the Lord, his obedience to the voice of God and his total commitment to fulfil the will of God moved the Lord's heart. Abraham had passed the test and the angel of the Lord called out of heaven the second time with a message from God: Genesis 22:17 That in blessing I will bless thee, and in multiplying, I will multiply thy seed as the stars of heaven, and as the sand which is upon the seashore and thy seed shall possess the gate of his enemies.

May Jesus be for ever glorified. Abraham slew a lamb for the burnt offering. Jesus was slain on calvary's cross and his blood shed to redeem man. Today he has possessed the gates of his enemies.

- Abraham obeyed God. Genesis 22:18 And in thy seed shall all the nations of the earth be blessed…

- Jesus obeyed his Father. Philippians 2:9-11 Wherefore God also hath highly exalted him and given him a name that is above every name. 10. That at the name of Jesus every knee should bow, of things in heaven, and things in earth, and things under the earth; 11. And that every tongue should confess that Jesus Christ is Lord, to the glory of God the Father.

Mother W's testimony

It was Sunday evening and we were travelling to church. The other sisters were discussing the things of God and I was praying. When we got to a certain point I stopped praying and joined the other sisters in discussing heavenly things.

When we reached church I became very unwell. I somehow felt very weak and my strength seemed have ebbed away. Darkness came over me and I called out, "Please get me out of the car, I am not feeling well".
This they did. I felt the pangs of death come over me.

Sisters J and P pleaded the blood of Jesus. They cried out loudly, "the blood of Jesus, the blood of Jesus, the blood of Jesus". Sister P called out to Jesus to help and began to bind the spirit of death which was over me. They hoped that other saints would arrive to help them to deliver me. [We were early and the first to get to church on this particular evening]. Thank God other brethren began to arrive and they all joined in the fight for my life. They pleaded the blood of Jesus from deep in their spirits until I came round. By the time Apostle Lake arrived I was already on my feet. She did not seem in the least disturbed by what had happened but told us that the Lord had given us a deeper revelation of the power in the blood of Jesus.

I thank God for the teaching that Apostle Lake had given us on the blood of Jesus Christ. I have experience of its life giving power. It is the blood that brought me back to life. Had it not been for the precious blood of Jesus which my Christian sisters pleaded, I felt I might have died. Praise God for the precious blood of Jesus.

I can recommend the blood of Jesus for every condition of life that could come upon anyone. Jesus' blood, saves, heals, delivers from demons and raises the dead. To Jesus be all the praise and glory. Leviticus 17:11 For the life of the flesh is in the blood…

CHAPTER 6

LEADING UP TO THE EXODUS

Genesis 12:1-3 1. Now the Lord had said unto Abram, Get thee out of thy country and from thy kindred, and from thy father's house, unto a land that I will show thee. 2. And I will make of thee a great nation, and I will bless thee, and make thy name great; and thou shalt be a blessing. 3. And I will bless them that bless thee, and curse him that curseth thee: and in thee shall all families of the earth be blessed.

God called Abram from Ur of the Chaldees. Abram left his father's house as the Lord had said to him. He took his nephew Lot along with him and his wife Sarai and travelled out. When Abram got to the plain of Moreh the Lord appeared unto him. Genesis 12:7 And the Lord appeared unto Abram, and said, Unto thy seed will I give this land: and there builded he an altar unto the Lord, who appeared unto him.

Abram understood the importance of blood sacrifice. When the Lord visited him here, he builded an altar unto the Lord. On these altars animal sacrifices were offered. The Lord cut a covenant with Abram as he travelled out and told him that his seed, through whom all the nations of the earth would be blessed, would become strangers in a land that would not be theirs, they would serve that nation who would afflict them four hundred years, but the Lord promised to bring them out of their bondage.

Genesis 15:13-14 13. And he said unto Abram, know of a surety that thy seed shall be a stranger in a land that is not theirs, and shall serve them; and they shall afflict them four hundred years: 14. And also that nation whom they shall serve, will I judge: and afterward shall they come out with great substance.

I will continue to say that God is a covenant keeping God. He made a covenant with Abram and promised to bring his descendants out of bondage in due time. After the covenant was cut with Abram, God changed his name to Abraham, "for a father of many nations have I made thee" [Genesis 17:5]. Abraham's son Isaac, heir of the promise, was born and was circumcised, to fulfil the will of God.

Ishmael, Abraham's son by Hagar, the Egyptian, took a wife of the people around him but Abraham, in his old age, gave a firm command to the servant of his house and made him swear to it by the God of heaven that he would not take unto Isaac a wife of the daughters of the Canaanites among whom he dwelt. Abraham commanded his servant to go to Abraham's family and take a wife from amongst them for his son Isaac. God's people should not mix with the idolators. Abraham's servant took ten camels and rode off to Mesopotamia with Abraham's blessing. God was working out his will.

Abraham's servant met up with Rebekah, the daughter of Abraham's nephew. This was in the plan of God. Rebekah came to the well to draw water. In answer to the prayer of Abraham's servant, she gave him water to drink and also watered his camels. God's will was fulfilled. She took him home to meet her family who approved her marriage to Isaac. Rebekah returned with

Abraham's servant and became the wife of Isaac. [Read Genesis 24 for detailed account].

In process of time, Esau and Jacob [twins] were born to Isaac and Rebekah. There were problems in the family. Esau sold his birthright to Jacob for a pot of soup. Besides this, their mother helped Jacob deceive his father into giving Jacob the blessing that belonged to the firstborn. Obviously, Esau was very hurt, although Isaac did give Esau a blessing also. Genesis 25:27-34 27. And the boys grew, and Esau was a cunning hunter, a man of the field; and Jacob was a plain man, dwelling in tents. 28. And Isaac loved Esau, because he did eat of his venison: but Rebekah loved Jacob. 29. And Jacob sod pottage; and Esau came from the field and he was faint: 30. And Esau said to Jacob, Feed me I pray thee with that same red pottage, for I am faint; therefore was his name called Edom. 31. And Jacob said, Sell me this day thy birthright. 32. And Esau said, Behold I am at the point to die; and what profit shall this birthright do to me? 33. And Jacob said, Swear to me this day; and he swear unto him: and he sold his birthright unto Jacob. 34. Then Jacob gave Esau bread and pottage of lentils; and he did eat and drink, and rose up; and went his way; thus Esau despised his birthright.

Genesis 27:1-4, 6, 7, 9-10 1. And it came to pass, that when Isaac was old and his eyes were dim, so that he could not see, he called Esau his eldest son, and said unto him, My son; and he said unto him, Behold, here am I. 2. And he said, Behold now I am old and know not the day of my death: 3. Now therefore take, I pray thee, thy weapons, thy quiver and thy bow, and go out to the field and take me some venison. 4.And make me some savoury meat that I may eat; that my soul may bless thee before I die. 6. And Rebekah spake unto Jacob her son saying, Behold I heard thy father speak unto Esau thy brother saying, 7.Bring me venison and make me savoury meat that I may eat and bless thee before I die. 9. Go now to the flock and fetch me from thence two good kids of the goats and I will make them savoury meat for thy father such as he loveth. 10. That he may bless thee before his death.

The chapter goes on to tell us how much Esau hated Jacob. The family bitterness was so great that Esau had plans to kill Jacob his brother. His mother was told and she called Jacob and sent him away to his uncle Laban. [Genesis 27:42-43]

God had plans for Jacob's life. His mother seemed to have been trying to help God in bringing about his plans. She made a terrible mistake because in so doing she brought great hatred between the brothers and lots of problems for Jacob. We must allow God to do his work in his own way because his ways are past finding out.

Esau was a very weak person because he sold out his inheritance quite lightly to his deceitful brother. There is a price to pay for sin and Jacob would find this out in time.

Jacob went off, as instructed by his mother to his uncle Laban. His father gave him his blessing. Isaac did not want his sons to take wives of the heathen women and he advised Jacob to take himself a wife of his father's house. Genesis 28:3-4 3. And God Almighty bless thee, and make thee fruitful, and multiply thee, that thou mayest be a multitude of people. 4. And give thee the blessing of Abraham, to thee, and to thy seed with thee…

As a man sow, so shall he also reap [Galatians 6:7]. Jacob would receive what he had given to his brother. His uncle Laban would see to that. Laban deceived Jacob in the matter of his wife. He worked for seven years for Rachel but his uncle Laban gave him Leah and he had to work another seven years for Rachel. His uncle Laban changed his wages ten times. However, God was with him and had great plans for his life. God blessed him and prospered him greatly at Padan-aram. When the time came for him to return home he left with great substance. God promised to bless Jacob and he kept his promise.

Genesis 28:11-14 11.And he lighted upon a certain place and tarried there all night. 12. And he dreamed and behold a ladder set up on the earth and the top of it reached to heaven, and behold the angels of God ascending and descending on it. 13. And behold the Lord stood above it, and said, I am the Lord God of Abraham thy father, and the God of Isaac: the land whereon thou liest to thee will I give it, and to thy seed. 14. And thy seed shall be as the dust of the earth, and thou shalt spread abroad to the west, and to the east, and to the north, and to the south: and in thee and in thy seed shall all the families of the earth be blessed. God's plans will be fulfilled and whatever happens in-between will not stop God's purposes from coming to pass.

God wanted Jacob back home and Jacob was also missing home. Jacob therefore ran away from his uncle Laban, taking with him his two wives, Leah and Rachel, the two nurse maids, the children God had given him in Padan-aram and the great substance of animals with which the Lord had blessed him. His uncle Laban chased him and caught up with him, although he could do nothing to him because Jacob was in the plan of God.

Jacob reached home safely and was reconciled with his brother Esau. God gave him twelve sons by his two wives and their maids.

Rachel, Jacob's first love, was barren for a long time whilst Leah her sister and Rachel's maid were bearing children unto Jacob.God remembered Rachel and opened her womb [Genesis 30:22]. Joseph was the first son that Rachel bore to Jacob and Jacob loved him dearly. This was to cause problems in the family. His brothers hated him. Jacob loved Joseph so much he gave him a coat of many colours. The coat and Joseph's dreams turned his brothers against him and they hated him bitterly. Genesis 37:6-8 6. And he said unto them, Hear, I pray you, this dream which I have dreamed. 7. For, behold, we were binding sheaves in the field, and lo, my sheaf arose, and also stood upright; and behold your sheaves stood round about, and made obeisance to my sheaf.

Joseph told his dream to his parents and they realized he would, at some point in time, be above his brothers, although they rebuked him because it seemed they would also be bowing down to him.

Joseph's brothers had plans to kill him out of envy. He fell into their hands when Jacob sent him to see how they were doing with the flock in Shechem. Because Joseph was in the plan of the Lord, instead of killing him, God allowed Joseph to be sold into Egypt. The brothers deceived their father by putting animal blood upon Joseph's coat and they also deceived their father into believing that an animal had slain Joseph. Obviously, the news brought great sorrow to the heart of Jacob; he mourned the death of his son. The brothers thought to do Joseph evil but God would work it out that Joseph had gone before them to preserve their lives in time of famine.

Joseph was sold to Potiphar, Pharaoh's officer and captain of the guard. Joseph was loved and made ruler over Potiphar's house. His wife also loved Joseph with a carnal love and when Joseph refused to get in line with her carnal desires she had him sent to prison. God blessed Joseph whilst in prison. With God's mark upon Joseph, he prospered even in the prison house and when Pharaoh could find no one to interpret his dream, Joseph was recommended to the king, whereupon he interpreted the dream, which had to do with a forthcoming famine.

Joseph was promoted in Egypt and only the king was greater than Joseph. Pharaoh gave Joseph the job of organizing storage of food in preparation for the forthcoming famine. As the famine raged over the entire then known world, Jacob sent his sons to Egypt to buy food. The story says that when they got to Egypt to buy food the person in charge was Joseph whom the brothers did not recognize. Joseph remembered them and enquired after his father and his brother Benjamin. Joseph was determined to see his mother's other son, his younger brother. Simeon was bound and thrown in prison until Benjamin was brought down to Egypt. It was a very terrible thing to expect Jacob to send Benjamin down with the brothers to Egypt. After all, they had had Joseph slain by wild beasts? There would be no more food forthcoming until Benjamin was brought down. Jacob gave in and sent Benjamin along with the brothers.

Joseph was extremely pleased to see his younger brother. He sent much food for his father, his brother Benjamin was safe, Simeon was released and Joseph wept. His father was brought down to Egypt and there was a wonderful re-union as the king of Egypt gave the land of Goshen to Jacob and his children where they could be at peace in Egypt and be fed, they and their animals. Everything was fine as long as Joseph remained alive.

Israel's children prospered and multiplied in Egypt and they became very great. Only seventy persons went down to Egypt during the time of famine. Now there were thousands of people.

Joseph died and the new kings did not know Joseph, nor his people and they made slaves of the children of Israel. They brought them into hard bondage. They were in bondage for some 400 years in accordance with the prophecy of the Lord. The children of Israel cried unto the Lord and they continued to cry. The Lord remembered his covenant with Abraham, Isaac and Jacob and he came down to deliver them. Exodus 3:7-8 7. And the Lord said, I have surely seen the affliction of my people which are in Egypt, and have heard their cry by reason of their taskmasters: for I know their sorrows; 8.And I am come down to deliver them out of the hand of the Egyptians, and to bring them up out of that land unto a good land and large, unto a land flowing with milk and honey….

When the Lord has his hand on your life, none of the obstacles that come your way will hinder God's plans for your life. The Lord will watch over you like he did Joseph and you will come out of your Egyptian bondage with great substance.

The Israelites were in the plan of God, so are you. They suffered for centuries but God was still working in their behalf and he is doing the same for you right now. Receive it in the name of Jesus.

My testimony by Sister J

Praise the Lord. I had been waiting for a very long time to have my immigration status sorted out. I came to the Apostolic Church of God 7th Day Ministries seeking help. I just loved the church and as a backslider I really wanted to return to the Lord. However, I was living with someone outside of marriage and we wanted to get married so I could get baptized. I was not hearing from the Immigration Department. I asked Apostle Lake to pray for me every time I attended church. I was desperate, I wanted to serve the Lord properly. Apostle Lake prayed and told me that God would sort out my immigration difficulties because I wanted to serve the Lord.

To God be all the glory and praise. I have received a letter from the Immigration Department advising me that I have been given leave to stay in the UK. There were many lovely things in the letter. I was allowed to travel, work and live as a lawful citizen.

I have seen many miracles at the Apostolic Church of God 7th Day Ministries and I have also received my miracle. What can I say? If you want to be saved, healed, delivered from demons, find a wife or husband, get your immigration problems sorted out and whatever else, come to the Apostolic Church of God 7th Day Ministries and receive your prayers of deliverance. I can recommend this ministry. Jesus is here and may the Lord continue to bless our church and ministry.

CHAPTER 7

WHEN I SEE THE BLOOD I WILL PASS OVER YOU

Exodus 12:1-13 1. And the Lord spake to Moses and Aaron in the land of Egypt saying, 2. This month shall be unto you the beginning of months; it shall be the first month of the year to you. 3. Speak unto the congregation of Israel, saying, In the tenth day of this month they shall take to them, every man a lamb, according to the house of their fathers, a lamb for an house: 4. And if the household be too little for the lamb, let him and his neighbour next unto his house take it according to the number of the souls; every man according to his eating shall make your count for the lamb. 5. Your lamb shall be without blemish, a male of the first year; ye shall take it out from the sheep or from the goats; 6. And ye shall keep it up until the fourteenth day of the same month; and the whole assembly of the congregation of Israel shall kill it in the evening. 7.And they shall take of the blood and strike it on the two side posts and on the upper door post of the houses, wherein they shall eat it. 8. And they shall eat the flesh in that night, roast with fire, and unleavened bread; and with bitter herbs they shall eat it. 9. Eat not of it raw, nor sodden at all with water, but roast with fire; his head with his legs, and with the purtenance thereof. 10.And ye shall let nothing of it remain until the morning; and that which remaineth of it until the morning ye shall burn with fire. 11. And thus shall ye eat it; with your loins girded, your shoes on your feet, and your staff in your hand, and ye shall eat it in haste: it is the Lord's passover. 12. For I will pass through the land of Egypt this night, and will smite all the firstborn in the land of Egypt, both man and beast; and against all the gods of Egypt I will execute judgement: I am the Lord. 13. And the blood shall be to you for a token upon the houses where ye are, and when I see the blood, I will pass over you, and the plague shall not be upon you to destroy you, when I smite the land of Egypt.

Moses was born to be a leader of God's people. God preserved him in the river and took him out of the ark of bulrushes and placed him in Pharaoh's palace via Pharaoh's daughter. Exodus 2:1-6 1. And there went a man of the house of Levi, and took to wife a daughter of Levi. 2. And the woman conceived and bare a son: and when she saw him that he was a goodly child, she hid him three months. 3. And when she could no longer hide him, she took for him an ark of bulrushes, and daubed it with slime and with pitch, and put the child therein; and laid it in the flags by the river's brink. 4.And his sister stood afar off to wit what would be done to him. 5. And the daughter of Pharaoh came down to wash herself at the river, and her maidens walked along by the river's side, and when she saw the ark among the flags, she sent her maid to fetch it. 6. And when she had opened it, she saw the child, and behold, the babe wept. And she had compassion on him, and said, This is one of the Hebrews' children.

According to the king's command, Moses should have been killed. The new Pharaoh had ordered all the boys born to the Hebrew women to be killed. He was very concerned at the increase in number of the Hebrews in his country and they seemed to be very prosperous. He might have found out that there were only seventy of them when the children of Israel first settled in Egypt and now there were many thousands of them. He wondered whether they would take over the country. The midwives who were to destroy the boy babies saved them because they feared God. Moses' mother knew of the king's command, looked at her lovely baby and thought, "no way". She hid him in the river, in the plan of God, to be found by the king's daughter, to be brought up in the palace to learn [without Moses being aware of it], how to rescue his people from their hard bondage.

Somehow, Moses retained his heritage and he was well aware of who he was. He saw the sufferings of his people and assisted one of the Hebrews who had a fight with an Egyptian. Moses killed the Egyptian. Exodus 2:11-15 11.And it came to pass in those days, when Moses was grown, that he went out unto his brethren, and looked on their burdens: and he spied an Egyptian smiting an Hebrew, one of his brethren. 12. And he looked this way and that way, and when he saw that there was no man, he slew the Egyptian, and hid him in the sand. 13. And when he went out the second day, behold two men of the Hebrews strove together: and he said to him that did wrong, Wherefore smitest thou thy fellow? 14. And he said, Who made thee a prince and a judge over us? intendest thou to kill me, as thou killedst the Egyptian? And Moses feared, and said, Surely this thing is known. 15. Now when Pharaoh heard this thing, he sought to slay Moses. But Moses fled from the face of Pharaoh and dwelt in the land of Midian: and he sat down by a well.

The Lord was on Moses' side despite such a difficult situation.

Moses met up with the priest of Midian who gave him one of his daughters to marry. More than that, Moses met up with God. God needed to talk with Moses, who was born to fulfil the great plan of God in bringing Abraham's decendants out of Egyptian bondage. God, could not, however, talk with Moses in Egypt, he needed to come out.

Moses kept the flock of his father-in-law Jethro. He had to learn how to lead the flock. God called Moses out of the fire. Exodus 3:2-8, 10. 2. And the angel of the Lord appeared to him in a flame of fire out of the midst of a bush; and he looked and behold the bush burned with fire, and the bush was not consumed. 3. And Moses said, I will now turn aside, and see this great sight, why the bush is not burned. 4. And when the Lord saw that he turned aside to see, God called unto him out of the midst of the bush and said, Moses, Moses. And he said, Here am I. 5. And he said, Draw not nigh hither: put off thy shoes from off thy feet, for the place whereon thou standest is holy ground. 6. Moreover he said, I am the God of thy father, the God of Abraham, the God of Isaac, and the God of Jacob. And Moses hid his face; for he was afraid to look upon God. 7. And the Lord said, I have surely seen the affliction of my people which are in Egypt, and have heard their cry by reason of their taskmasters: for I know their sorrows; 8. And I am come down to deliver them out of the hand of the Egyptians, and to bring them out of that land unto a good land and a large, unto a land flowing with milk and honey; unto the place of the Canaanites, and the Hittites, and the Amorites, and the Perizzites, and the Hivites, and the Jebusites. 10. Come now therefore, and I will send thee unto Pharaoh, that thou mayest bring forth my people, the children of Israel out of Egypt.

In our sufferings and in our difficult times we often do not realize that God may well have a great call on our lives. The greater God's call on our lives, it seems the greater the suffering. Suffering cleans us up, purges us out of all the impurities, toughens us up, humbles us, and gets us at the place where God can use us. In Moses' case he ran away, alas, to the place where God could meet him. The mandate was given, however, Moses had no plans for this, and came up with excuses. The Lord told Moses; I will be with thee! [Exodus 3:12]. Moses' faith wavered and he said, "Lord they will not believe you have sent me". They will ask: "What is his name?". "Tell them, I AM hath sent thee"

The Lord told Moses to gather together the elders of Israel and tell them he had seen their affliction, and in keeping with his promise, he had come to deliver them, and they would believe him. Then said the Lord, take the elders with you and go to Pharaoh and tell him: ..."The Lord God of the Hebrews hath met with us: and now let us go, we beseech thee, three days' journey into the wilderness that we may sacrifice to the Lord our God" [Exodus 3:18]. Moses insisted that they would not believe him. Exodus 4:2-3 2. And the Lord said unto him, What is that in thine hand? And he said, A rod. 3. And he said, Cast it on the ground. And he cast it on the ground, and it became a serpent; and Moses fled from before it. [Exodus 4:2-3]. The Lord was working miracles to help Moses believe, a stick had become a snake. His hand had become leprous when he put it in his bosom, at the command of the Lord, when Moses took his hand out of his bosom the leprosy had disappeared. If the Israelites do not believe the first sign said the Lord to Moses, they will believe the second sign which Moses would demonstrate. Now go, the Lord told him.

May the Lord help us to stop doubting the power of God. What must God do to make us believe? More excuses! I am not an eloquent speaker declared Moses to the Lord, as if God did not know that. I am confident the king of Egypt understood Moses' words whilst he was in the palace. I will give you your brother Aaron to be your mouthpiece, said the Lord to Moses. God is so patient with our weaknesses. Aaron will speak what I will tell you. You will be the leader and Aaron will say what you tell him, from me. Now go, and take the rod with you because you will do signs with it. God finally got through to Moses, praise his wonderful name. Can you see yourself here. We all want to work for the Lord, but we get so scared when he gives us tasks, and doubts flood into our spirits, all about our shortcomings.

We often forget that it is God who will work through us to do his good pleasure.

Moses finally got the message from the Lord and went back to his father-in-law Jethro and took leave of him to return to Egypt. Go in peace, said Jethro. The Lord told Moses that all those who sought to kill him were dead and Moses took his wife and children and the rod of God and set off for Egypt.

God's blood covenant must be kept. This is of utmost importance. Something drastic happened along the way. Moses neglected to circumcise his son. Exodus 4:24-26
24. At a camping place on the way to Egypt, the Lord met Moses and tried to kill him. 25-26. Then Zipporah, his wife, took a sharp stone, cut off the foreskin of her son, and touched Moses' feet with it. Because of the rite of circumcision she said to Moses, "You are a husband of blood to me". And so the Lord spared Moses' life

[GNB]. We see how important the blood covenant of circumcision was; God would have killed Moses. His plan must not be spoilt through our neglect, he would rather move us out of the way. His will must be done. Praise the Lord. At the time the covenant of circumcision was drawn up by the Lord, he told Abraham that the uncircumcised man child whose flesh of his foreskin was not circumcised, that soul would be cut off from his people; "he hath broken my covenant".

Genesis 17:14]. The penalty for breaking this blood covenant was death, despite the fact that Moses was called of God to undertake such a great task. The word of God stands fast forever. Obedience is the answer. Zipporah quickly circumcised the child.

Moses met up with his brother Aaron, whose heart the Lord had prepared, and they went together to Egypt to bring the Lord's people out of bondage. What was to follow typifies our escape out of the kingdom of darkness into God's marvelous light. If we are determined to be wicked, God can help us to be even more wicked in order that he may punish us. The word says that the Lord hardened Pharaoh's heart. [Exodus 7:3].

Moses went in to Pharaoh with Aaron his brother. He used the rod of God to do signs. The plagues and signs run in this order:

- Moses cast down his rod before Pharaoh at the command of the Lord. The rod became a serpent [snake]. The king called for his magicians and sorcerers who cast down their rods as well. Praise the Lord, there is no god like our God. Moses' serpent [rod] swallowed up theirs,

God's power is far superior. Satan and his demons are under the feet of the Lord's people.

- The river became blood as Moses struck it, in the presence of Pharaoh, with the rod of God. All waters in Egypt turned into blood. There was blood all over Egypt.

  God's mighty power is again magnified in the eyes of the heathen.

- Frogs covered Egypt as Aaron stretched the rod out over the rivers, canals and pools at the command of the Lord. The frogs went up out of the rivers, canals and pools and into the palace, the homes, even in their cooking vessels.

  The hand of God was everywhere.

- Lice was all over Egypt as the Lord commanded Moses to tell Aaron to strike the ground with the rod and cause the dust to become lice. The lice was everywhere. The magicians said to the king, "the Lord has done this" because they tried to make lice appear also, but they failed.

  Satan and his demons will be allowed of God to go only so far, praise his wonderful name.

- Flies were sent by the Lord into Pharaoh's palace and on the king himself and all his officials. The land was full of flies. At this point the king half-heartedly called for Moses and Aaron and told them to sacrifice to the Lord in Egypt. Obviously, Moses and Aaron refused. "We must travel three days into the wilderness to sacrifice to our God".

Church we must not do service/sacrifice to our God in the enemy's territory. We must come out of Egypt and be clear of it completely.

Go three days in the wilderness to sacrifice to your God, said the king, but don't go far, and pray for me that the flies leave us. Moses prayed. The Lord removed the flies, but the king was hardened.

Don't go far said the devil. Satan would like the church to stay near the world. Forget it devil.

- The animals died. The Lord sent a terrible disease on all the animals that belonged to the Egyptians and they died. The Lord saved the animals of the Israelites.

  God will take care of his people, and the righteous will not perish with the wicked.

- Boils came up on the Egyptians. The Lord told Moses and Aaron to take a few handfuls of ashes from a furnace and throw these into the air. The ashes will spread out like fine dust all over the country [the land of Goshen, where the Israelites lived was exempted] which will produce boils on all the Egyptians and their animals.

  Again, God's people were not included in the destruction.

- Hail fell on the whole of Egypt as Moses raised his hand toward the sky at the Lord's command. The hail fell and lightening flashed. It destroyed all the plants and broke all the trees. This took place everywhere in Egypt except in Goshen where the Lord's people lived.

  It is exciting to see how God takes care of his people.

- Locusts filled the palace and the homes of all Pharaoh's officials. The locusts ate all that the hail had not destroyed. The land was ruined. The king's officials pleaded with him to let the people go so that the hand of the Lord would be withdrawn from Egypt, but the king was hardened. [Exodus chapters 9 and 10].

The message from the Lord to Pharaoh, "Let my people go that they may sacrifice to me" was loud and clear but the king was unable to hear it. The signs spoke out, but he could not see them! Pharaoh was waiting for the fulfilment of the word of God upon him and his people.

- **The slaying of the lamb – the tenth sign**

The tenth sign would be a very dangerous one and God would make special provision to protect his people. There were several lessons to be learned from this sign. Pharaoh had asked Moses to pray that the Lord would remove the plagues previously, but this time prayer would not help, death was hanging over Egypt, including the heir to the king's throne. There would be wailing in Egyptian households; their firstborn sons would be killed. The hand of God was stretched out over Egypt for destruction. The king would be so hard hit that he would drive the Israelites from his presence.

God remembered his promise to Abraham; he would bring his descendants out of Egyptian bondage. Abraham had offered the blood sacrifices necessary when the covenant was cut.

The Lord's people had been crying out to God for deliverance from their taskmasters over centuries and the time for their freedom had come. Their dead situation would come alive by the use of the blood. The blood would be a mark/seal upon the homes of the Israelites and the destroying angel would pass over them. The blood of a lamb would be very significant, representing the blood of the Lamb of God who takes away the sins of the world. St John 1:29 The next day John seeth Jesus coming unto him and saith, Behold the Lamb of God which taketh away the sin of the world. The blood of the lamb would also typify the Lamb that was slain from the foundation of the world Revelation 5:6,12 6. And I beheld, and lo, in the midst of the throne and of the four beasts, and in the midst of the elders, stood a Lamb as it had been slain, having seven horns and seven eyes…12. Saying with a loud voice, Worthy is the Lamb that was slain, to receive power and riches, and wisdom and strength, and honour, and glory, and blessing.

The deliverance is in the blood of the slain lamb. The Lord's people were to get a lamb for each house. If the lamb was too much for a small household, they were to share it with the next door neighbour in proportion to the number of people and the amount each person could eat.. [Then Jesus said unto them: Except ye eat the flesh of the Son of man and drink his blood, ye have no life in you –

St John 6:53]. They could use either a sheep or a goat of a year old which had to be without defect. That was very important because holiness combats sin. On the God given day, the fourteenth day of the month Abib in the evening, the whole community of Israel would kill the animals. The blood was extremely important: to seal, mark off and deliver the people. They were commanded to put the blood on the doorposts, above the doors of the houses in which the animals were to be eaten. The meat was to be roasted whole [we must receive all of Christ] including the head, legs and internal organs, and none of it should be left until the next day. If any was left over it should be burnt. It should be eaten quickly, they were to be dressed for travel with their sandals on their feet and their stick in their hands.

On that night the destroying angel would pass through the land of Egypt, killing every first born male, both human and animal and the Lord would punish all the gods of Egypt. The blood on the doorposts would be a mark to signify that they were the Lord's people and when the destroying angel saw the blood he would pass over them, and they would be under the Lord's safety covering. The protection on the houses was the blood.

The whole Egyptian nation wept bitterly that night as their eldest son, beginning at Pharaoh's palace was killed. The hand of God was against them. They did not have the mark of the blood over their homes. Their family did not eat the flesh of the lamb and were exposed to the destroying angel.

The whole family ate the lamb. As the blood was placed on the house, the whole family was covered. When Jesus shed his blood, he covered all who believed and their households. The blood of Jesus is in the holiest and remains there to meet our needs. Jesus took his blood there himself. Hebrews 9:12 Neither by the blood of goats and calves, but by his own blood he entered in once into the holy place, having obtained eternal redemption for us.

Have you got unsaved children? Bring them by faith into the house and cover your house with the blood of Jesus. They are included in the blood and the meat. How do I do this? you ask. By faith, plead the blood of Jesus. How? Say, "the blood of Jesus to bring my son into this house, the blood of Jesus to save him, the blood of Jesus to protect him. I daub the blood of Jesus on my front door, on the doorposts, on the windows; I pour out the blood of Jesus on the floor and on the ceiling".

When you bring them in by the blood of Jesus, cause them to receive the life of God with the blood of Jesus. Speak these words over them: Leviticus 17:11 The life of the flesh is in the blood; and I have given it to you upon the altar to make an atonement for your souls: for it is the blood that maketh an atonement for the soul. You then plead the blood of Jesus to drive out the demons: "the blood of Jesus, the blood of Jesus, the blood of Jesus" Demons fear and tremble when you plead the blood of Jesus aloud. It tells the story of the liberation of God's people, by the type and reality, and the reality is Christ. The sound of the blood of Jesus cripples the demons. Not only so, pleading the blood of Jesus will wake up the dead spirits of your children and they will become alive and respond to the gospel message positively. The sound of the blood of Jesus will cleanse the hearts of sin and satan and his works. Plead the blood of Jesus.

Jesus' blood is in the holy place waiting to connect up with your voice as you shout out loudly "the blood of Jesus".The mention of the blood of Jesus becomes poison to satan and his demons, life to sinners, anointing and blessing to believers and rejoicing to heaven as it stands in awe and adoration of our precious Lord and saviour, Jesus Christ, the captain of our salvation. Plead the blood of Jesus.

The liberation of the Israelites from Egypt was only the shadow of our deliverance from sin and satan, the world, the flesh and the devil. God demonstrated his great power in signs and wonders upon Pharaoh and the Egyptians, he went to great lengths to bring his people out of bondage. God has gone to the greatest lengths, in giving his only beloved Son, to save the world from sin by the shedding of his precious blood.

Acts 16:31 Believe on the Lord Jesus Christ and thou shalt be saved and thy house.

The great Apostle Paul had the revelation of the exodus from Egypt. He understood about the "lamb for an house" and the blood, covering the houses of God's people for protection, so when he was leading the Philippian jailor to salvation in the Lord Jesus Christ, he said, "Believe on the Lord Jesus Christ and thou shalt be saved and **thy house**." He realized that the whole family was included, under the blood covering. Paul baptized all who were in the house that night, after he had spoken the word of God unto them. Cover your family with the blood of Jesus; they come under the blood.

CHAPTER 8

HOW THE BLOOD OF JESUS CHRIST BROUGHT NAOMI BACK TO LIFE

It was Sabbath morning. I travelled down with Evangelist Fullerton [my son-in-law] to minister in the Brixton fellowship. Our practice is to plead the blood of Jesus as we enter the church. This we did for some time and the service went on as usual. The Holy Spirit blessed us all and we went home rejoicing.

My son-in-law drove us back to his home where I had left my car. We got out of his car in the normal manner and I rang the door bell as usual, so that I could pop in and have a hot drink before going home. My grand-daughter, 12 years old, came to open the door. Her greeting this time was "Naomi died in church today" [Naomi was 10 years old at the time; the daughter of Evangelist Blake. They attend the Wembley branch of the ministry, which is pastored by my eldest daughter, Pastor Judy, wife of Evangelist Fullerton]. Naomi, what? I asked, absolutely thrown by this news. "She died in church today", my grand-daughter repeated. Evangelist Fullerton quickly intervened: What did you say? By this time I was speechless and felt like a cord had run around my stomach. "She died, but they pleaded the blood of Jesus and she came back to life", Charmaine [my grand-daughter] said. What a relief!

"Go on, tell us what happened today", we implored my daughter as we entered the living room. She was waiting for us. She related it as follows:

We got to church in the normal way. Evangelist Blake came in early with Naomi and the two boys. He had set up the musical instruments and whilst we were pleading the blood of Jesus, he tapped me on my shoulder and said, "I am going to pick up Michaela. Back soon". We continued pleading the blood of Jesus for sometime. We covered by faith the ceilings of the building, the chairs, the windows, the floors, the doorposts, the lintels, all the instruments and vessels that we use in the church. We sprinkled the blood of Jesus on all the saints, by faith. We sprinkled the bibles and song books with the blood of Jesus and we began to worship the Lord. The presence of the Lord was awesome in the place.

Naomi was seated on a chair next to where Estella was standing. [Estella is a trained/fully qualified nurse]. Naomi seemed to have fallen off the chair onto the floor. Carmen [usher] saw what had happened and ran over to her. She put Naomi on her lap as she sat on the floor. [Carmen works with disabled children and is first class at first aid treatment]. However, Naomi seemed to have stretched out on Carmen's lap.

Everything was happening so quickly. Teacher Max and I were called as Carmen screamed out loudly. Estella did what a qualified nurse is taught to do, but said there was nothing more she could do to help. Sister Max and I began to plead the blood of Jesus. Naomi's eyes turned white and her tongue stuck out. I alerted the whole congregation to plead the blood of Jesus. I remembered all you had taught us about the life of the flesh being in the blood and decided never to let up until she came round. We pleaded the blood of Jesus from the bottom of our hearts. Everyone cried out, "the blood of Jesus, the blood of Jesus, the blood of Jesus". The life had gone out of Naomi but we believed we could bring her back to life by applying the blood of Jesus. She would just have to come round. I would have felt very guilty if she hadn't come round. How could I face her dad. I felt responsible. Vern [Naomi's mum] had left for the Caribbean on Friday, the day before Naomi died, to attend the tombing of her mother. How could I ever break such awful news to her. We persevered and just pleaded the blood of Jesus and trusted the Lord completely. Sister Annette [best friend of Naomi's mother] took the microphone and walked up and down the church pleading the blood of Jesus.

I pushed Naomi's tongue back in her mouth and tried straightening up her distorted face. After about 10/15 minutes Naomi came round, looking very dazed. Naomi's father had to return to church because of the heavy traffic he had to contend with on his way to collect Michaela. He had telephoned his eldest daughter and asked her to take care of her little sister until he came home from church. By the time he had got to the church, Naomi had come back to life. He saw the congregation of God's people pleading the blood of Jesus with their whole heart so he drew near to see what had happened, only to find that it was his daughter who had died, although he had not long left her in good health. He took her up and carried her outside to get some fresh air, but Sister Annette continued to plead the blood of Jesus. Annette remembered what you said about Conrad, how when you stopped pleading the blood of Jesus, he slipped away faster than at the first. She also remembered that you said we should plead the blood of Jesus until the person had completely recovered. Annette pleaded the blood of Jesus for quite some time after Naomi had come round, just to be sure she was going to be all right.

Mum, it was a day we will never forget. The teaching you gave us sunk in and we received experience from this great miracle. Thank God for Jesus. We spent the rest of the day praising the Lord. Jesus is so worthy.

Someone had called the ambulance but by the time it came Naomi had started to play. They checked her and found nothing wrong. However, "we will take her down to the hospital for some tests" they said. This they did. The hospital discharged her as being in perfect health. "Tell daddy what you told me" said Rachel [Naomi's older sister] to Naomi.

When I was on the floor a man with black eyes, very short and with brown hair, took hold of my hand, spun me around and said, "you are coming with me, you are coming with me". During this time I heard the words, "the blood of Jesus, the blood of Jesus", the blood of Jesus". Those were the only words I heard and I woke up.

Pastor Judy told me she was binding the spirit of death, but when she remembered that I had said I did that when Conrad [her brother] had died, and he said he had not heard those words, [only the words "the blood of Jesus"] she went back to pleading the blood of Jesus.

I [Apostle Lake] must thank God again for another great miracle. The Lord has never left me alone and he has never caused me to be put to shame. I taught the church what the Lord had revealed to me and Jesus had confirmed his word with signs and wonders. Plead the blood of Jesus.

If you have a dead situation in your life, plead the blood of Jesus over it: sickness, unruly children, a bad husband, a bad wife, a poorly paid and boring job, examination difficulties, inability to read and understand the word of God and pray, confusion of mind, wicked neighbours, witchcraft powers over your life and evil speakers; plead the blood of Jesus. If you keep getting held up on the roads and keep missing your train so that you are often late for work and an important appointment, plead the blood of Jesus, the demons are crossing your wire and destroying your plans: Get going: the blood of Jesus, the blood of Jesus, the blood of Jesus. Jesus has revealed this to me, I have taught it to our ministers and saints at home and abroad and it works, praise the Lord.

Exodus 24:6-11, 17 6. And Moses took half of the blood and put it in basins; and half of the blood he sprinkled on the altar. 7. And he took the book of the covenant, and read in the audience of the people: and they said, All that the Lord hath said will we do, and be obedient. 8. And Moses took the blood, and sprinkled it on the people, and said, Behold the blood of the covenant, which the Lord hath made with you, concerning all these words. 9. Then went up Moses and Aaron, Nadab and Abihu, and seventy of the elders of Israel: 10. And they saw the God of Israel: and there was under his feet as it were a paved work of a sapphire stone and as it were the body of heaven in his clearness. 11. And upon the nobles of the children of Israel he laid not his hand: also they saw God, and did eat and drink. 17. And the sight of the glory of the Lord was like devouring fire on the top of the mount in the eyes of the children of Israel.

It is Jesus' blood that brings us into the presence of the Lord where his glory and beauty can be seen. In verse 5 of Exodus chapter 24 we see that Moses sent young men of the children of Israel to offer burnt offering and to sacrifice peace offerings of oxen unto the Lord. The sacrifice was about the blood of the animals which would be shed. After the sacrifice the blood was sprinkled upon the altar. Moses then read the book of the covenant to the people. [The blood opened the door to the reading of the book of the covenant to the people]. Once the word got to the people, Moses sprinkled them with the blood of the covenant which the Lord had made with them.

It was after Moses and his co-workers had ministered the blood that they saw the glory of the God of Israel.

Hebrews 9:18-26 18. Whereupon neither the first testament was dedicated without blood. 19. For when Moses had spoken every precept to all the people according to the law, he took the blood of calves and of goats with water and scarlet wool, and hyssop and sprinkled both the book and all the people, 20. Saying, This is the blood of the testament which God hath enjoined unto you. 21. Moreover he sprinkled with blood both the tabernacle and all the vessels of the ministry. 22. And almost all things are by the law purged with blood, and without shedding of blood is no remission. 23. It was therefore necessary that the patterns of things in the heavens should be purified with these; but the heavenly things themselves with better sacrifices than these. 24. For Christ is not entered into the holy places made with hands, which are the figures of the true; but into heaven itself, now to appear in the presence of God for us: 25. Nor yet that he should offer himself often, as the high priest entereth into the holy place every year with blood of others; 26. For then must he often have suffered since the foundation of the world: but now once in the end of the world hath he appeared to put away sin by the sacrifice of himself.

When Jesus went back to heaven after defeating satan at the cross, he took his own blood into the most holy place where it remains. When we say, “the blood of Jesus, the blood of Jesus”, we connect up with Christ’s blood in the most holy place and Jesus’ blood cries out loud and clear, “the price has been paid, here it is; satan has no right to offend them”. The demons and satan himself smell the fires of hell and must therefore let go of the situation and free us up and release us from our problems. Pour out Jesus’ blood, by faith, on every condition. The blood of Jesus speaks.

Saints, Moses poured out the blood of animals on all the vessels of the ministry. Plead the blood of Jesus. The blood was also sprinkled on the people. Pastors, sprinkle the congregation with the blood of Jesus and drive the demons out of the church. If animal blood served to bring God’s people into his presence, under the Old Testament, how much more will the blood of Jesus Christ serve to bring the church into the most holy place under the New Testament. Hebrews 10:19 Having therefore boldness to enter into the holiest by the blood of Jesus . The church can be bold to enter into the holiest. The blood of Jesus says “Yes” to our deliverance. This is a new and living way, praise the Lord.

Thank God we do not need to kill animals [in the old way], we just need to plead the blood of Jesus. Jesus has made things so easy for us. We are very blessed with the use of the blood of Jesus. All we have to do is to speak the words, by faith, and it is done.

Leviticus 4:13-21 13. And if the whole congregation of Israel sin through ignorance, and the thing be hid from the eyes of the assembly, and they have done somewhat against any of the commandments of the Lord, concerning things which should not be done, and are guilty; 14. When the sin, which they have sinned against it is known then the congregation shall offer a young bullock for the sin, and bring him before the tabernacle of the congregation. 15. And the elders of the congregation shall lay their hands upon the head of the bullock before the Lord: and the bullock shall be killed before the Lord. 16. And the priest that is anointed shall bring of the bullock's blood to the tabernacle of the congregation: And the priest shall dip his finger in some of the blood, and sprinkle it seven times before the Lord, even before the veil. 18. And he shall put some of the blood upon the horns of the altar which is before the Lord, that is in the tabernacle of the congregation and shall pour out all the blood at the bottom of the altar of the burnt offering, which is at the door of the tabernacle of the congregation. 19. And he shall take all his fat from him, and burn it upon the altar. 20. And he shall do with the bullock as he did with the bullock for a sin offering, so shall he do with this: and the priest shall make an atonement for them, and it shall be forgiven them. 21. And he shall carry forth the bullock without the camp, and burn him, as he burned the first bullock: it is a sin offering for the congregation.

It is of note that the anointed priest should bring the bullock's blood to the tabernacle of the congregation. We, the church are a royal priesthood. …" [1 Peter 2:9] But ye are a chosen generation, a royal priesthood, an holy nation, a peculiar people. Revelation 1:6 And hath made us kings and priests unto God and his Father; to him be glory and dominion forever and ever, Amen.

The use of the blood of Jesus is not for everyone. It is for the use of those who have been saved by his blood. Ephesians 1:7. In whom we have redemption through his blood, the forgiveness of sins. Those who have been redeemed by Christ's blood and carry the anointing of priesthood [by salvation] are qualified to use the blood of Jesus to fight spiritual battles.

The blood should be sprinkled by the anointed priest seven times [we should sprinkle the blood of Jesus upon our lives every day, seven days/week]. The priest should sprinkle the blood before the Lord, before the veil. Leviticus 4:6 And the priest shall dip his finger in the blood, and sprinkle of the blood seven times before the Lord, before the veil of the sanctuary. The blood was sprinkled before the veil. The precious blood of Jesus would tear open that veil from the top to the bottom giving us access by his blood into the holiest. Matthew 27:51-52 51. And behold the veil of the temple was rent in twain from the top to the bottom; and the earth did quake and the rocks rent, 52. And the graves were opened, and many bodies of the saints which slept arose.

The veil, under the Old Covenant was very significant and so was the altar on which some of the blood had to be put. The altar had to be sanctified because that is where we lay our burdens down and meet with God. Pour out Jesus' blood, by faith, at the altar. Now, kneel down and pray and God will meet you there.

CHAPTER 9

THE BLOOD BRINGS THE FIRE DOWN – ONLY FOR THE PEOPLE OF GOD

1 Kings 18:19-39 [GNB] 19. Now order all the people of Israel to meet me at Mount Carmel. Bring along the 450 prophets of Baal and the 400 prophets of the goddess Asherah who are supported by Queen Jezebel. 20. So Ahab summoned all the Israelites and the prophets of Baal to meet at Mount Carmel. 21. Elijah went up to the people and said, "How much longer will it take you to make up your minds. If the Lord is God worship him; but if Baal is God, worship him!" But the people didn't say a word. 22. Then Elijah said, I am the only prophet of the Lord still left, but there are 450 prophets of Baal. Bring two bulls; let the prophets of Baal take one, kill it, cut it in pieces, and put it on the wood – but don't light the fire. I will do the same with the other bull. 24. Then let the prophets of Baal pray to their god and I will pray to the Lord, and the one who answers by sending fire – he is God. The people shouted their approval. Then Elijah said to the prophets of Baal, Since there are so many of you, you take a bull and prepare it first. Pray to your god, but don't set fire to the wood. 26. They took the bull that was brought to them, prepared it and prayed to Baal until noon. They shouted, Answer us Baal, and kept dancing round the altar they had built, but no answer came. 27. At noon Elijah started making fun of them: Pray louder, he is a god! Maybe he is day-dreaming or relieving himself, or perhaps he is gone on a journey! Or maybe he is sleeping and you've got to wake

him up! 28. So the prophets prayed louder and cut themselves with knives and daggers according to their ritual, until blood flowed. 29. They kept on ranting and raving until the middle of the afternoon; but no answer came, not a sound was heard.

30. Then Elijah said to the people, Come closer to me, and they all gathered round him. He set about repairing the altar of the Lord, which had been torn down. 31. He took twelve stones, one for each of the twelve tribes, named after the sons of Jacob, the man to whom the Lord had given the name Israel. 32. With these stones he rebuilt the altar for the worship of the Lord. He dug a trench round it, large enough to hold almost fourteen litres of water. Then he replaced the wood on the altar, cut the bull in pieces, and laid it on the wood. He said, Fill four jars with water and pour it on the offering and the wood. They did so, 34. And he said, Do it again, and they did. Do it once more, he said, and they did. 35. The water ran down round the altar and filled the trench. 36. At the hour of the afternoon sacrifice the prophet Elijah approached the altar and prayed, O Lord, the God of Abraham, Isaac and Jacob, prove now that you are the God of Israel and that I am your servant and have done all this at your command. 37. Answer me, Lord, answer me, so that this people will know that you, the Lord are God, and that you are bringing them back to you. 38. The Lord sent fire down, and it burnt up the sacrifice, the wood, and the stones, scorched the earth and dried up the water in the trench. When the people saw this, they threw themselves on the ground and exclaimed, The Lord is God; the Lord alone is God!

King Ahab was a very wicked king. As if he was not evil enough he married Jezebel the daughter of a heathen king, Ethbaal of Sidon. The Lord had told the Israelites not to marry into the heathen nations who would turn their hearts away from him. At that time the people worshipped idols and further rebelled against the Lord by practicing witchcraft. The Lord sent Elijah to meet with Ahab during the time of a terrible famine. The Lord had purposed to turn the nation back to himself. The king and the queen had turned them away from the Lord by their wickedness. The Lord had used Elijah to prophesy that there would be famine in the land and that there would be no rain for some three years [1 Kings 17:1]. The time had come when the Lord would send rain, and the prophet Elijah was sent by the Lord to advise King Ahab of this.

King Ahab and one of his palace officials, Obadiah, were going through the land trying to find grass to keep the animals alive. On his way to find Ahab Elijah met with Obadiah who greeted him, and Elijah asked Obadiah to go and tell King Ahab that he [Elijah] had come to see him. Obadiah was a righteous man who rescued and hid one hundred of the Lord's prophets and fed them with bread and water. He had hid them in caves to protect them from Jezebel who was killing the Lord's prophets. Obadiah expressed his fear of taking the message to Ahab. He felt that whilst he was gone, Elijah would disappear and he would be left to face the wrath of King Ahab, who would kill him. Elijah promised Obadiah that he would not disappear but would be there to meet Ahab.

Obadiah took the message to King Ahab who came to meet Elijah. "Here you are, you trouble-maker in Israel". King Ahab greeted Elijah. "I am not a trouble-maker, you are, because by your wickedness you have turned the people's hearts away from God, and you are worshipping the idols of Baal. Arrange for all the people to meet me at Mount Carmel and bring along the 450 prophets of Baal and the 400 prophets of the goddess Asherah who Queen Jezebel supports".King Ahab did as Elijah requested. He ordered the Israelites and the prophets of Baal to meet Elijah at Mount Carmel.

I believe Elijah took a good look at these idolaters and witchcraft workers. "How long is it going to take you to make up your minds? If God be God, serve him, but if Baal be God serve him". The people did not respond. I am the only prophet of the Lord here, said Elijah, and the prophets of Baal are many.

God had a work to do that day in turning the hearts of the people back to him, in repentance. The rain could not fall whilst the rebellion remained and the witchcraft and idolatry continued. The land needed to be cleansed. The reason there was no rain and there was famine was because the nation had lived in disobedience to the word of God, and the condition needed to change.

Reading through Chapter 18 of 1st Kings we find that when the heathens could get no answer from their gods, they cut themselves until blood gushed out. Satan loves the shedding of human blood. Not so with Elijah. He repaired the altar of the Lord that had been broken down, he restored the foundation which sin had destroyed. He used twelve stones, representing the twelve tribes of the children of Israel. God is a covenant keeping God and this stood to remind the Lord of his covenant promises with Abraham, Isaac and Jacob [Israel]. Then came the offering of the animal sacrifice. The bull was cut in pieces and placed on the wood on the altar. To bring the fire down there had to be a blood sacrifice, offered by a holy servant of the Lord. The blood sacrifice of the heathen was insignificant because they were not holy before the Lord and any blood sacrifice they offered would only work negatively. God will hear the voice of his people who walk righteously before him and he will defend them. The Lord has promised that the righteous man will never be put to shame.

Elijah offered his prayer at the time of the evening sacrifice. At that time Elijah acknowledged the supremacy of God. We must know how to move God. 1 Kings 18:36-37 36. O Lord, the God of Abraham, Isaac and Jacob, prove now that you are the God of Israel and that I am your servant and have done all this at your command. 37.Answer me Lord, answer me, so that this people will know that you, the Lord are God and you are bringing them back to yourself.

There was a great difference between the two altars. The altar of the heathen was an ordinary altar. The altar of Elijah was extraordinary. Jars of water was poured on Elijah's altar, so much water was poured out that it ran down round the altar and filled up the trench. Normally, when anything is as wet as that altar it would be very difficult to light it up. I believe God was very pleased with the faith of Elijah, which was at an all time high. Despite all that water that might have got mixed in with the blood from the bullock, the blood brought the fire of the Lord down and consumed the sacrifice.

The blood of Jesus, through our sacrifice of praise offered up to God, in righteousness, will bring the fire of the Holy Ghost down. The qualification to use the blood of Jesus with good success is righteousness; walking in obedience to the commandments of the Lord. Those people walking in disobedience are never assured success in using the blood of Jesus. Are you walking in line with the word of God? Plead the blood of Jesus.

What happened when the people saw the fire?

When the people saw the fire of the Lord, they cried out, The Lord is God, the Lord alone is God. The sacrifice brought the people to the place of repentance. Before the rain of the Holy Spirit will fall, sin has to be taken out of the way through repentance and confession of faith.

The Lord sent rain in Israel and took away the drought and famine after :

- The blood sacrifice was offered according to the plan of God;
- The people had acknowledged who was the true God [theLord, he is God];
- The prophets of Baal had been killed [the cause of the problem removed].

Is there drought and famine in your Christian walk?

Search for the sin in your life and offer your blood sacrifice on the repaired altar of the Lord. How do I do this? Repent and confess your sins before the Lord. Ask his forgiveness on the merits of his shed blood only, and thank him for your deliverance.

Time for the rain 1 Kings 18:44-45 Elijah ordered his servant; 44. Go to King Ahab and tell him to get into his chariot and go home before the rain stops him. 45. In a little while the sky was covered with dark clouds, the wind began to blow, and heavy rain began to fall. [GNB]

James 5:17-20 17. Elias was a man subject to like passions as we are, and he prayed earnestly that it might not rain: and it rained not on the earth by the space of three years and six months. 18. And he prayed again, and the heaven gave rain, and the earth brought forth her fruit. 19. Brethren, if any of you err from the truth, and one convert him, 20. Let him know that he which converteth the sinner from the error of his way shall save a soul from death, and shall hide a multitude of sins.

So you say Elijah was a prophet called of the Lord, that's why he could pray that no rain would fall and no rain fell. The bible says that because we are cleansed by the blood of the Lord Jesus Christ, from all our sins and are born again and have become new creatures in Christ, we can ask God for whatever we desire, in the name of Jesus and we will receive it. We can do what Elijah did and more because we have been brought back to the first dominion of power and authority by the blood of Jesus. Elijah prayed seven times before the rain fell. We must keep praying and speaking to the situation on the merits of the shed blood of Jesus Christ and victory is ours.

Ephesians 1:22-23 22. And hath put all things under his feet, and gave him to be the head over all things, to the church; 23. Which is his body, the fullness of him that filleth all in all.

The blood of the bull brought down the fire of God in Elijah's ministry and turned the people's hearts back to God. The blood of Jesus is much more powerful to disperse the powers of darkness and make good things happen in our lives and ministries.

Let me give this testimony

I remember very well the year we were ministering in the Philippines. Rain began to fall. It fell for days. The water rose to the steps we walked up, to go into the house in which we stayed. It came into the rooms. The courtyard was all covered with water which was quite deep. When we stepped into the water to go out it was up to our waist. I said to the pastors, We need to pray because the buses and other means of transportation had stopped running and most people, including ourselves were housebound. We came together in a prayer meeting and cried out to the Lord. I, personally, commanded the rain to cease in the name of Jesus. We stood firm on the word of God which we read aloud. We then praised the Lord and worshipped. We all went off to bed in the very wet house, and slept. The next morning we woke up to find that the rain had ceased, the thunder and lightening had also ceased, the water at the front of the house had almost dried up, and by mid-morning the buses were running again. What Elijah did was available to us through the shed blood of our Lord Jesus Christ.

Evangelist D's testimony

I knelt down and began to pray as usual. The Holy Spirit led me to pray for each member of our church, a mammoth task. However, I remembered Pastor Lake telling us to pray the blood of Jesus, since the blood of Jesus tells the full redemption story. I began by taking the name of each member and ministering the blood of Jesus over their household. I prayed like this: I plead the blood of Jesus over Sister P's household. I send the blood of Jesus into her bedroom to wash it out and cleanse it. I did this to each room as the Holy Spirit led me. What I saw I will never forget. I saw a pool of blood flowing up the stairs and flowing into each room.

The blood was washing the rooms as I prayed. I did not realize the blood [running substance] could flow up the stairs, but it did. The scripture, ..with God all things are possible [Matthew 19:26] became very real to me and I knew then that the blood of Jesus is truly full of life.

I saw inside the rooms in the spirit although physically I had never been in those rooms and I was truly amazed at what I saw the living blood of Jesus doing. The blood did just what I had prayed. To God be all the glory and praise.

I began to pray for another member of our church and pleaded the blood of Jesus over her home, and the same thing happened. It was really happening. I took my own family and prayed the blood of Jesus over their rooms. I saw the blood travelling up our stairs into each bedroom as I called them by name. The blood was flowing through and through and cleansing each room. It was a sight to behold, praise the Lord Jesus. Now, I plead the blood of Jesus over every situation and I pray the blood of Jesus. I send out the blood of Jesus and ask it to do things to help people. From my experience the blood of Jesus, prayed by the Lord's people, do what it is asked to do. It is a living tool for evangelism. It makes things happen.

To Christian leaders, workers and saints I say, plead the blood of Jesus over difficult situations and pray the blood of Jesus. It will make all the difference; the blood of Jesus works for God's people.

Sister M's testimony

I used to be involved in witchcraft. My son was ill. I did not know the Lord and I needed help, so I went to any occultist I was told may be able to help. I travelled to various places to see these people; distance and aircrafts were not a problem.

During my time of worry and desperation someone told me about Jesus. I gave my heart to the Lord and got baptized. However, the church I attended did not understand many of my problems. The witch-doctors had made my son's condition worse and I suffered from terrible fear. Each witch-doctor seemed to have added more difficulties. I began to see all sorts of insects in front of me and I felt I would be out of my mind if I did not receive deliverance from these evil spirits.

I was invited to the Apostolic Church of God 7th Day ministries. I attended the Brixton branch where Apostle Lake ministered. They prayed without ceasing at this ministry. I was advised to attend the Wednesday evening deliverance meetings. I went through about four sessions of deliverance prayers and things started to get better. Apostle Lake told me to plead the blood of Jesus if the evil spirits tried to come back.

On a particular evening I left the service as usual and headed for home. Some evil spirits decided to travel in front of me and I was very afraid. I remembered the teaching Apostle Lake gave the church on the blood of Jesus and I began to plead the blood of Jesus. As I pleaded the blood of Jesus: "the blood of Jesus, the blood of Jesus, the blood of Jesus", I saw a pool of blood flowing in front of me. It went ahead of me until I got home and then disappeared. I was rather surprised because I did not understand that the blood of Jesus could appear in such a natural way, flowing in front of me and leading me home. I just praised the Lord when I got home safely.

Thank God for the blood of Jesus. It is real. When you have problems, plead the blood of Jesus. When demons come to attack you, plead the blood of Jesus. I plead the blood of Jesus over every adverse condition that satan puts on me. It works. To Jesus be all the praise and all the glory.

CHAPTER 10

OUR PRAYERS MUST BE MIXED WITH THE BLOOD OF JESUS

2 Chronicles 6:12-14, 18-21, 26-31 12. And he [Solomon] stood before the altar of the Lord in the presence of all the congregation of Israel, and spread forth his hands. 13. For Solomon had made a brazen scaffold, of five cubits long and five cubits broad, and three cubits high, and had set it in the midst of the court: and upon it he stood, and kneeled down upon his knees before all the congregation of Israel, and spread forth his hands toward heaven. 14. And said, O Lord God of Israel, there is no God like thee in heaven, nor in the earth; which keepest covenant, and shewest mercy unto thy servants, that walk before thee with all their hearts: 18. But will God in very deed dwell with men on the earth? behold, heaven and the heaven of heavens cannot contain thee; how much less this house which I have built. 19. Have respect therefore to the prayer of thy servant, and to his supplication, O Lord my God, to hearken unto the cry and the prayer which thy servant prayeth before thee: 20. That thine eyes may be open upon this house day and night, upon the place whereof thou hast said that thou wouldest put thy name there; to hearken unto the prayer which thy servant prayeth toward this place. Hearken therefore unto the supplications of thy servant, and of thy people Israel, which they shall make toward this place: hear thou from thy dwelling place, even from heaven: and when thou hearest, forgive.

26. When the heaven is shut up, and there is no rain, because they have sinned against thee; yet if they pray toward this place, and confess thy name and turn from their sin, when thou dost afflict them; 27. Then hear thou from heaven, and forgive the sin of thy servants, and of thy people Israel, when thou hast taught them the good way, wherein they should walk; and send rain upon thy land which thou hast given unto thy people for an inheritance. 28. If there be dearth in the land, if there be pestilence, if there be blasting, or mildew, locusts or caterpillars; if their enemies besiege them in the cities of their land, whatsoever sore or whatsoever sickness there be; 29. Then what prayer or what supplication soever shall be made of any man, or of all thy people Israel, when everyone shall know his own sore and his own grief, and shall spread forth his hands in this house: 30. Then hear thou from heaven thy dwelling place, and forgive, and render unto every man according unto all his ways, whose heart thou knowest; [for thou only knowest the hearts of the children of men:] 31.That they may fear thee, to walk in thy ways, so long as they live in the land which thou gavest unto our fathers.

The Lord laid it upon the heart of his servant King David to build the Lord a house where the ark of the covenant could rest, and where the Lord could put his holy name. King David had shed much blood in wars, and even under the Old Covenant the Lord would not allow him to do so, although David would have been delighted to build this house for the Lord. However, the Lord chose Solomon [David's son by Bathsheeba, the wife of Uriah the Hittite] to build it.

2 Chronicles 28:2-3, 5-6 2. Then David the king stood up, upon his feet, and said, Heaı me my brethren, and my

people: As for me, I had in my heart to build an house of rest for the ark of the covenant of the Lord and for the footstool of our God, and had made ready for the building: 3. But God said unto me, Thou shalt not build an house for my name, because thou hast been a man of war, and hast shed blood. 5. And of all my sons [for the Lord hath given me many sons] he hath chosen Solomon my son to sit upon the throne of the kingdom of the Lord over Israel. 6. And he said unto me, Solomon, thy son, he shall build my house and my courts: for I have chosen him to be my son, and I will be his father.

When Solomon was crowned in the place of his father David, "a man after God's own heart" [Acts 13:22....to whom also he gave testimony, and said, I have found David the son of Jesse, a man after mine own heart..."] he was young and it pleased the Lord that he had asked him for wisdom, knowledge and understanding to rule the people. There is something very revealing here. On a particular night the Lord appeared to Solomon and asked him what he would like the Lord to give him. Before Solomon went to bed he went up to the brazen altar before the Lord and offered a thousand burnt offerings upon it. Solomon had a thousand animals killed and burnt whole upon the altar. Can you imagine how much blood would have been poured out of these animals. It was a very big sacrificial offering. Much blood was shed. This offering pleased the Lord.

2 Chronicles 1:6-12 [GNB] 6. In front of the tent, the king worshipped the Lord by offering sacrifices on the bronze altar; he had a thousand animals killed and burnt whole on it. 7. That night God appeared to Solomon and asked, What would you like me to give you? 8. Solomon answered, You always showed great love to my father

David, and now you have let me succeed him as king. 9. O Lord God, fulfil the promise you made to my father. You have made me king over a people who are so many that they cannot be counted, 10. So give me the wisdom and knowledge I need to rule over them. Otherwise, how would I ever be able to rule this great people of yours? 11. God replied to Solomon, You have made the right choice. Instead of asking for wealth or treasure or fame or the death of your enemies, or even for long life for yourself, you have asked for wisdom and knowledge so that you can rule my people, over whom I have made you king. 12. I will give you wisdom and knowledge, and in addition I will give you more wealth, treasure and fame than any king has ever had before or will ever have again.

Can you see what animal blood did? The quantity of offering that Solomon made showed the wholeness of his heart towards God and the Lord accepted the powerful blood sacrifice. How much more will the blood of Jesus please the Lord when we offer it up by confession? All we need to do is plead the blood of Jesus by faith, from a humble and a contrite heart. We can enter into the holiest by pouring out the precious blood of Jesus. After King Solomon's whole-hearted blood sacrifice, he received from the Lord much more than he had asked for. Solomon was now equipped to build the Lord's house.

God has made his ministers kings and priests and like King Solomon we will need to offer up our blood sacrifice [the blood of Jesus] to receive anointing of wisdom, knowledge and understanding like the Lord gave to Solomon in order that we may build the house of our God.

In accordance with God's call upon King Solomon's life, he built the house of the Lord on Mount Moriah, where the Lord appeared to his father David, in the place that David had prepared, in the threshing floor of Araunah the Jebusite. [2 Chronicles 3:1]. King David had made all the preparation for the building and he gave the plans for all the temple buildings to Solomon. He also gave him the plans for the courtyards and the rooms around them. He gave Solomon the plans for organizing the priests and Levites to perform their duties. He gave instructions as to how much silver and gold was to be used for making the temple utensils, for each lamp and lampstand, the amount of gold for making forks, bowls, jars etc. David also gave Solomon instructions as to how much pure gold was to be used to make the altar on which incense was to be burnt. David made it as easy as possible for his young son to do what he would have liked to do, that is, building an house for the Lord.

Solomon was brought up in a righteous home. His father was a king/priest who had great revelations of the mysteries of the kingdom of God. He wrote many Psalms, some of which prophesied of the coming of Christ. Solomon knew the importance of blood sacrifices and he poured out his heart to the Lord in the quality and quantity of his blood sacrifices.

The building of the house of the Lord had come to an end. I believe King David would have been most happy to have lived to see the completion of the house of the Lord. King Solomon got the nation of Israel together and prayed one of the most powerful prayers of dedication and submission to the Lord. He touched, by the Spirit of the Lord, all the areas of life where the people could go wrong and he asked the Lord to forgive them if they prayed either in the temple or towards the temple. I will touch only a few of the many things King Solomon prayed about in 2 Chronicles chapter 6, and for which he asked the Lord's forgiveness if they would either pray in the house of the Lord or towards the house of the Lord:

- If a man sinned against his neighbour;
- If thy people be put to the worse before their enemies;
- When the heaven is shut up and there is no rain because the people have sinned;
- If there is no rain because the people have sinned;
- If there is famine in the land or an epidemic;
- If there be scorching winds destroying the crops;
- If there is sickness amongst the people;

King Solomon asked the Lord to hear the prayers of the people if they kneel before him in the temple and prayed. He asked the Lord to forgive and help them. King Solomon acknowledged that their problems would be due to the disobedience of the people to the Lord's commands.

[King Solomon asked the Lord to watch over the temple day and night].

Solomon asked the Lord to hear the prayer of foreigners who would hear of his greatness and come to the house of the Lord to pray. He also asked the Lord to hear the prayer of his people if they prayed to him from another country where he had allowed them to be taken captive by their enemies because of their rebellion against the Lord.

It is very important to offer the blood sacrifice before prayers and that was what Solomon did. Plead the blood of Jesus before you start to pray. This takes you into the direct presence of God. The blood removes the demons out of the way and brings the fire down. Plead the blood of Jesus.

2 Chronicles 7:1-6 1. And when Solomon had made an end of praying, the fire came down from heaven and consumed the burnt offering and the sacrifices, and the glory of the Lord filled the house. 2. And the priests could not enter into the house of the Lord, because the glory of the Lord had filled the house. 3. And when all the children of Israel saw how the fire came down, and the glory of the Lord upon the house, they bowed themselves with their faces to the ground upon the pavement, and worshipped, and praised the Lord saying, For he is good; for his mercy endureth for ever. 4. Then the king and all the people offered sacrifices before the Lord. 5. And King Solomon offered a sacrifice of twenty-two thousand sheep; so the king and all the people dedicated the house of God. 6. And the priests waited on their offices, the Levites also with instruments of music of the Lord which David the king had made to praise the Lord, because his mercy endureth for ever, when David praised by their ministry; and the priests sounded trumpets before them, and all Israel stood.

Solomon had slain the animals and had burnt them whole upon the altar. The burnt offering was very significant as a type. The blood was shed and the animal was offered – burnt whole. We must be wholly sacrificed to the Lord. Christ's blood has been shed and our whole sin self must be burnt on the altar. Solomon prayed on behalf of the whole Israelite congregation. He had met the Lord's requirement under the Old Covenant. Down came the fire of God and consumed the sacrifices. The anointing came down so heavily that the priests could not enter the temple. The awesome holiness of God filled the temple. The people fell prostrate at the Lord's feet in worship and adoration. The blood of those sacrifices brought the Holy Ghost fire down.

Here is more revelation: After the fire came down, in answer to the prayers, King Solomon offered an even greater sacrificial offering of thousands of animals; blood flowed. Some of the sacrifices had to be offered in the courtyard, [there was so much of it], and the people praised the Lord as the priests and Levites stood in the places assigned to them.

After King Solomon had set everything in order in the house of the Lord, the Lord appeared to him by night in regard to the nation of Israel and concerning prayers made at the temple.

The blood sacrifices offered before the prayers brought the anointing down for worship and service; the blood sacrifices after the prayers, brought the answers down.

2. Chronicles 7:11-22 [GNB] 11. After King Solomon had finished building the temple and the palace, successfully completing all his plans for them, 12. the Lord appeared to him at night. He said to him, I have heard your prayer, and I accept this temple as the place where sacrifices are to be offered to me. 13. Whenever I hold back the rain or send locusts to eat up the crops, or send an epidemic on my people, 14. If they pray to me and repent and turn away from the evil they have been doing, then I will hear them in heaven, forgive their sins

and make their land prosperous again. 15. I will watch over this temple and be ready to hear all the prayers that are offered here, because I have chosen it and consecrated it as the place where I will be worshipped forever. I will watch over it and protect it for all time. 17. If you serve me faithfully, as your father David did, obeying my laws and doing everything I have commanded you, 18. I will keep the promise I made to your father David when I told him that Israel will always be ruled by his descendants. 19. But if you and your people ever disobey the laws and commands I have given you, and worship other gods, 20. Then I will remove you from the land that I gave you, and I will abandon this temple that I have consecrated as the place where I am to be worshipped. People everywhere will ridicule it and treat it with contempt.

21. The temple is now greatly honoured, but then everyone who passes by it will be amazed and will ask, Why did the Lord do this to this land and this temple? 22. People will answer: It is because they abandoned the Lord their God who brought their ancestors out of Egypt. They gave their allegiance to other gods and worshipped them. That is why the Lord has brought this disaster on them.

Worship at the temple would be very significant and God would remember the prayer of King Solomon when Israel was in trouble.

Daniel knew about this, and when he was in trouble in Babylon, he kneeled down and turned towards Jerusalem and prayed. Daniel 6:10 Now when Daniel knew that the writing was signed, he went into his house; and his windows being open in his chamber toward Jerusalem, he kneeled upon his knees three times a day, and prayed, and gave thanks before his God as he did aforetime.

The woman of Samaria knew about the temple worship in Jerusalem, so she reminded Jesus that Jerusalem was the place where men ought to worship. St John 4:20 Our fathers worshipped in this mountain; and ye say, that in Jerusalem is the place where men ought to worship. Jesus taught her when she received the water of life that he would give her she would enter into spiritual worship.

Today, because Jesus died, we have his blood available to us wherever we are. It is no longer necessary to go up to Jerusalem to offer animal blood sacrifices, we can plead the blood of Jesus over our prayers and bring anointing to us and the answers to our prayers.

Plead the blood of Jesus .

Hebrews 10:19-22 19. Having therefore, brethren, boldness to enter into the holiest by the blood of Jesus, 20. By a new and living way, which he hath consecrated for us, through the veil, that is to say, his flesh; 21. And having an high priest over the house of God; 22. Let us draw near with a true heart in full assurance of faith, having our hearts sprinkled from an evil conscience, and our bodies washed with pure water.

Enter the presence of the Lord with boldness. You have the blood of Jesus!

Leviticus 16:14 And he shall take of the blood of the bullock and sprinkle it with his finger upon the mercy seat eastward; and before the mercy seat shall he sprinkle of the blood with his finger seven times.

Start sprinkling the blood of Jesus at the mercy seat and receive answers to prayers. You will need to sprinkle it every day.[seven days/week]. The blood of Jesus opens God's heart to our prayers.

2 Samuel 24:25 And David built there an altar unto the Lord, and offered burnt offerings and peace offerings. So the Lord was entreated for the land and the plague was stayed from Israel.

When King David numbered Israel and sinned against the Lord he offered animal sacrifices at the threshing floor of Araunah the Jebusite and appeased the anger of the Lord. Christian brothers and sisters, we can cause the plague to cease out of our lives as we plead the blood of Jesus in the presence of the Lord.

Use the blood of Jesus.

CHAPTER 11

GOD SO LOVED THE WORLD

St John 3:16 For God so loved the world that he gave his only begotten Son, that whosoever believeth in him should not perish but have everlasting life.

Man sinned, his life blood dried up and he died. God still loved him. That blood needed to be replaced to restore life unto man. God created all things by Jesus Christ [his word]. St John 1:1 In the beginning was the word and the word was with God and the word was God. Obviously, the blood that flowed through man at the beginning was the blood of Christ. Man was, therefore, cut off from the Lord and lost fellowship with God when he sinned. God is not a God of the dead and man needed to be brought back to life to find fellowship with God. The life of the flesh is in the blood. Man needed the blood that was lost when he disobeyed God to be replaced.

For a time God used animal blood to cover man's sin but this could not give him life. This sufficed for covering him, it would not do for the inner man. Animal blood could not be mixed with human blood. For life to enter man again he needed blood inside him. This blood would pay the price of his sin, cleanse his inner man and put life back into him.

What would God do? The entire universe was looking on. The angels wanted to know. Revelation 5:2-5 2. And I saw a strong angel proclaiming with a loud voice, Who is worthy to open the book and to loose the seals thereof? 3. And no man in heaven, nor in earth, neither under the earth, was able to open the book, neither to look thereon. 4. And I wept much, because no man was found worthy to open and read the book, neither to look thereon. 5. And one of the elders said unto me, Weep not: behold, the Lion of the tribe of Judah, the Root of David, hath prevailed to open the book and to loose the seven seals thereof.

Why was no one else found worthy? Because the blood to pay the price for man's redemption had to come from the perfect source. Man was sealed under sin, sickness and disease, oppression, depression, poverty, hate, bitterness, unbelief, doubt and fear, […I heard thy voice in the garden and I was afraid…Genesis 3:10] confusion and torment, death and hell. Man was doomed to die and end up in hell. There were seven seals that held man bound to destruction and the price to loose them could be paid by no-one apart from Jesus. The blood to pay the price for man's redemption had to be life-giving blood. Only God gives life so the blood had to come from him. Since man had sinned, man must pay the price required to take the legal rights away from the devil, hence God would have to put on flesh to condemn sin in the flesh.

The bible says there was great excitement in heaven as Jesus stepped forward to open the book and to loose the seals. Wrapped up in those seven seals and that book were the sufferings Christ would have to go through and the victory over sin and satan. There would have been very much to read in that book of how:

- the Messiah would be conceived by the Holy Ghost [Luke 1:31 And behold thou shalt conceive in thy womb, and bring forth a son and shalt call his name Jesus];

- the woman would be a virgin [Luke 1:34 Then said Mary to the angel, how shall this be, seeing I know not a man?];

- the child would be given by the Lord an earthly father for his earthly nurturing [Matthew 1:20-21 But while he thought on these things, the angel of the Lord appeared unto him in a dream, saying, Joseph thou son of David, fear not to take unto thee Mary thy wife; for that which is conceived in her is of the Holy Ghost. And she shall bring forth a son, and thou shalt call his name Jesus: for he shall save his people from their sins].

The whole plan of salvation by Christ coming to earth and shedding his blood to reconcile man to God must have been in that book. The child would be raised in this poor village family; would stand by Joseph in his carpentry trade until it was time for him to branch out into public ministry at the age of 30 years. He would go through circumcision and be blessed by Simeon according to the Jewish custom.

Was it going to be a "walk over" to redeem man? Not at all. Isaiah 53:5 But he was wounded for our transgressions, he was bruised for our iniquities, the chastisement of our peace was upon him and with his stripes we are healed. His agony in the garden of

Gethsemane would have been all there facing him as he opened the book. Luke 22:44 And being in an agony he prayed more earnestly: and his sweat was as it were great drops of blood falling down to the ground. He was going to have to pray and sweat it out. He would have been running down the pages of that book to see that at one point he would feel like he could not go on. Matthew 26:39 And he went a little further, and fell on his face and prayed saying: O my Father, if it be possible, let this cup pass from me, nevertheless not as I will, but as thou wilt. The weight of sin had seemed too heavy at that point.

Jesus was looking in a moment of time at how Judas would be kissing him as identification. St Mark 14:44-45 And he that betrayed him had given them a token, saying, Whomsoever I shall kiss, that same is he; take him, and lead him away safely. 45. And as soon as he was come, he goeth straightway to him, and saith, Master, Master; and kissed him. The book would have outlined Peter's denial of him on three occasions. Matthew 26:75 And Peter remembered the word of Jesus, which said unto him, Before the cock crow, thou shalt deny me thrice. And he went out, and wept bitterly.

There might have been flashes before Jesus' eyes, as he looked in that book, of the cruel beatings he would be subjected to in order that his blood may cover the whole of man's needs. Man's whole destiny was corrupted by the devil and every area of man's life was going to have to be covered by his holy and precious blood. It was going to be very painful.During his sufferings, the disciples he loved, [who had witnessed his many miracles, signs and wonders] would forsake him. Mark 14:50 And they all forsook him and fled. It was going to be a very lonely road.

There would be the hearings before the Jewish religious leaders, before Pilate and Herod. He would be brutally whipped and mocked. The price of his blood to ransom man was high. The load of sin was heavy. Matthew 26:67-68 Then did they spit in his face, and buffeted him; and others smote him with the palms of their hands, 68. Saying, Prophesy unto us, thou Christ, Who is he that smote thee? He could hear the cry of the multitude. Luke 23:21 But they cried saying, Crucify him, crucify him. Pilate would hand him over to them to be crucified, but not without whipping. Mark 15:15 And so Pilate willing to content the people, released Barabbas unto them and delivered Jesus , when he had scourged him, to be crucified. The type of whipping coming to him would cause much bleeding to cover his whole physical body and pay the price for the healing of all man's diseases. After the whipping he would be hit on the head. Mark 15:19 And they smote him on the head with a reed, and did spit upon him, and bowing their knees worshipped him. He would be very humiliated. The crown of thorns on his head would cause much bleeding and this blood would cover man's mind and intellect.

It looked tough going but would be worth it because of the Father's great love for mankind. The devil must be defeated and man must regain his position in God. He must be reconciled. Mark 15:17-18 And they clothed him with purple, and plaited a crown of thorns, and put it about his head, and began to salute him, Hail, King of the Jews.

As Jesus ran through the book and loosed the seals the many miracles and love he would minister to the people shone like a light before him. He would overlook their ingratitude as the words "Father forgive them for they know not what they do", would pour out from his loving heart. Luke 23:34 Then said Jesus, Father, forgive them; for they know not what they do. And they parted his raiment, and cast lots.

As Jesus continued reading, he saw himself being flogged as he walked up Mount Calvary's hill and more blood was flowing from him. The blood was falling on the earth so that all who would avail themselves of his blood that was shed would receive abundant blessings from crops cultivated in the earth. The blood would cause the soil to be a blessing to them and yield abundantly.

The burden of sin was so heavy that he would fall under the cross and Simon of Cyrene would be on time to help him carry it. Matthew 27:32 And as they came out they found a man of Cyrene, Simon by name: him they compelled to bear his cross. As they nailed him to his cross he saw himself between two criminals one of whom would ask him to remember him when he came into his kingdom. Jesus was looking forward to helping this man. The other criminal took sides with the devil who would be completely disgraced.

Jesus might have groaned in himself at the thought of the spear being pierced into his side, but there must have been great joy as the battle for man's complete deliverance from satanic bondage came to a close with Jesus as the mighty conqueror. St John 19:34 But one of the soldiers with a spear pierced his side, and forthwith came there out blood and water. Although the book was showing that it would be a lonely road, since the disciples would run away and his Father would look away from him, his mind was made up.

Jesus understood the Father's plan to restore paradise to man and give him back the authority he once had. His blood would do all of that. The shedding of his blood would give man access to the holiest. Hebrews 10:19-20 Having therefore, brethren, boldness to enter into the holiest by the blood of Jesus. 20. By a new and living way, which he hath consecrated for us, through the veil, that is to say, his flesh.

Satan would be at a loss to understand how dreadfully his plans had failed when the veil of the temple would be rent in two as darkness covered the land for hours, while a centurion would say: Truly this man was the Son of God. St Mark 15:39 And when the centurion which stood over against him, saw that he so cried out and gave up the ghost, he said, Truly this man was the Son of God.

There was rejoicing in heaven as Jesus decided to take on flesh and come down to earth to pay the price with his blood, of delivering man from the kingdom of darkness and putting satan under the church's feet

Revelation 5:8-14 8. And when he had taken the book, the four beasts and four and twenty elders fell down before the Lamb, having everyone of them harps and golden vials full of odours, which are the prayers of saints. 9. And they sung a new song saying, Thou art worthy to take the book, and to open the seals thereof: for thou wast slain and hast redeemed to us to God by thy blood, out of every kindred, and tongue, and people, and nation. 10. And hast made us unto our God kings and priests: and we shall reign on the earth. 11. And I beheld, and I heard the voice of many angels round about the throne, and the beasts and the elders: and the number of them was ten thousand times, ten thousand, and thousands of thousands; 12. Saying with a loud voice, Worthy is the lamb that was slain, to receive power and riches, and wisdom and strength, and honour and glory and blessing. 13. And every creature which is in heaven, and on the earth, and under the earth, and such as are in the sea, and all that are in them, heard I saying, Blessing and honour, and glory and power, be unto him that sitteth upon the throne and unto the Lamb forever and ever. 14. And the four beasts said Amen. And the four and twenty elders fell down and worshipped him that liveth forever and ever.

Jesus' blood was shed, the price was paid and we are now kings and priests. We have rulership positions. Because it was Jesus' blood that brought the church back to this place of authority, whenever we plead the blood of Jesus over any condition, the blood speaks the full story of our redemption and reminds the devil he has lost and the authority is now back with the people of God. It also tells the devil he must obey us and go away. The blood of Jesus is very alive and active and it works. The blood of Jesus is a tool of evangelism which God has given to the church and it is to be used.

The blood of Jesus speaks: Hebrews 12:24 And to Jesus the mediator of the new covenant, and to the blood of sprinkling, that speaketh better things than that of Abel. Speak the blood of Jesus over your situation and then sprinkle it. Moses sprinkled the book and all the people in Old Testament times under the Old Covenant. He used the blood of animals. We have the precious blood of Christ, which satan and his demons dread. Hebrews 9:19, 21 19. For when Moses had spoken every precept to all the people according to the law, he took the blood of calves and of goats, with water and scarlet wool, and hyssop, and sprinkled both the book and all the people. 21. Moreover, he sprinkled with blood both the tabernacle and all the vessels of the ministry. We should do the same with the blood of Jesus. We do this by faith.

Walk around your home, your church, and sprinkle the blood of Jesus. Sprinkle it and speak it on your children and on your home.

- The blood of Jesus cleanses us from all our sins. 1 John 1:7 But if we walk in the light, as he is in the light, we have fellowship one with another, and the blood of Jesus Christ his Son cleanseth us from all sin.

- The blood of Jesus is a cleansing agent. Use it.

- The blood of Jesus Christ is alive and powerful. It hears and it does what you ask it to do in the name of Jesus, providing you are walking in the will of God.

- The blood of Jesus has brought dead people back to life in our ministry. We pleaded the blood of Jesus.

- The blood of Jesus is power and it brings a blessing when used by the people of God.

Ensure that you are a king/priest of God by repentance, faith and holiness. This way you can reign with Christ and you have his authority to use the blood of Jesus to fight against the demons and have them running. Thank God for giving us Jesus, who has given us his blood for sure victory.

CHAPTER 12

CLARIFYING WHAT THE BLOOD DOES FOR YOU – PART 1

The blood saves
Isaiah 53:5; Ephesians 1:7

The blood gives life
Leviticus 17:11; St John 6:53-54

The blood heals
Isaiah 53:5; Leviticus 14:5-7

The blood gives peace
Colossians 1:20

- **The blood saves**

Isaiah 53:5 But he was wounded for our transgressions, he was bruised for our iniquities: the chastisement of our peace was upon him; and with his stripes we are healed.

Ephesians 1:7 In whom we have redemption through his blood, the forgiveness of sins, according to the riches of his grace.

Jesus was born for the purpose of saving man from sin and the consequences of sin. His blood had to be shed for man's deliverance. No one else was found worthy.

The prophets foretold his sufferings: the beatings, the insults; they foresaw his nail scarred hands. His wounded side tells the story of his agony and the price that needed to be paid for man's redemption. Luke tells us that Jesus sweated it out. Luke 22:44 And being in an agony he prayed more earnestly: and his sweat became as it were great drops of blood falling down to the ground. Matthew tells us the place was Gethsemane. Matthew 26:36 Then cometh Jesus with them unto a place called Gethsemane, and saith unto the disciples, Sit ye here while I go and pray yonder. Jesus agonized to save us by the shedding of his precious blood. His whole body was torn and blood flowed from all over him so that he may cover every area of our lives with his salvation. The Apostle Paul puts it in very clear words: Ephesians 1:7 In whom we have redemption through his blood, the forgiveness of sins.

In 2 Samuel chapter 24 the bible says that the Lord was angry with the Israelites and he stirred up David, to bring destruction upon them. David gave orders to Joab, his army commander, to go throughout the tribes of Israel and number the people. Joab pleaded with the king not to do this, without success. The king had made up his mind and Joab obeyed orders and did as he was commanded.

It took Joab and his officers over nine months to go through the country and number the people. They reported back to the king the total number of men capable of military service. King David had probably forgotten how the Lord had blessed him in winning many battles; it was not by his efforts, it was by the strength of the Lord. David loved the Lord. He realized he had done wrong and his conscience began to trouble him. He prayed. 2 Samuel 24:10 [GNB] I have committed a terrible sin in doing this! Please forgive me, I have acted foolishly.

2 Samuel 24: 11-17 [paraphrased] 11.The Lord sent Gad, David's prophet to the king with this message: Tell the king I am giving him three choices of punishment and I will do whichever he chooses: Three years of famine in the land; three months of fleeing from his enemies; or three days of an epidemic in the land. 13. Gad delivered the Lord's word to David. Think about it, he said, make your choice and let me know what you decide so I can return with your decision to the Lord. 14. I am in a desperate situation, said the king. I do not want man to punish me, let the Lord himself punish us because he is merciful. 15. So the Lord sent an epidemic throughout the land for the duration of time stated – 3 days. From one end of the country to the other the epidemic killed 70,000 people. 16. When the Lord's angel was about to destroy Jerusalem the Lord was moved with compassion and stopped the angel. It is enough, the Lord said. [God is so merciful]. The angel was by this time at the threshing place of Araunah, a Jebusite. 17. David saw the angel who was destroying the people and cried out, "I am guilty, I am the one who has done wrong. The people have done no wrong, you should punish me and my family".

The blood saves. The Lord sent Gad, the prophet, to David. 2 Samuel 24:18-25 [GNB] 18.. Go up to Araunah's threshing place and build an altar to the Lord. 19. David obeyed the Lord's command and went as Gad had told him. 20…Your Majesty, why are you here? To buy your threshing place and build an altar unto the Lord and stop the epidemic, David replied. 22. Take it your

Majesty, Araunah said, and offer to the Lord whatever you wish. Here are these oxen to burn as an offering on the altar; here are their yokes and the threshing boards to use as fuel. 23. Araunah gave it all to the king and said to him, May the Lord your God accept your offering. 24. But the king answered, No, I will pay you for it. I will not offer to the Lord my God sacrifices that have cost me nothing. And he bought the threshing place and the oxen for 50 pieces of silver. 25. Then he built an altar to the Lord and offered burnt offerings and fellowship offerings. The Lord answered his prayer, and the epidemic in Israel was stopped.

The epidemic ceased on the offering up of the blood sacrifice by King David. The blood saved Israel.

Plead the blood of Jesus, which is more powerful than animal blood, and save yourself from your epidemic.

- **The blood gives life**

Leviticus 17:11 For the life of the flesh is in the blood: and I have given it to you upon the altar to make an atonement for your souls: for it is the blood that maketh an atonement for the soul

St John 6:53-55 53. Then Jesus said unto them, Verily, verily, I say unto you, Except ye eat the flesh of the Son of man, and drink his blood, ye have no life in you. 54. Whosoever eateth my flesh and drinketh my blood, hath eternal life; and I will raise him up at the last day.
55. For my flesh is meat indeed, and my blood is drink indeed.

Nearly everyone knows that if someone has a disease which makes him anaemic, or if he has not been eating properly and his blood level goes down, he is likely to end up feeling very weak. The doctors would probably put him on a course of something that would build up his blood. His life and strength is in the blood. Little blood gives little strength.

In the first chapter of this book, I shared how the Lord revealed to me the power in his precious blood. That experience taught me that the blood of Jesus not only covers and protects us, it gives life. I also learned that in order for the blood to work, we cannot just know about the blood of Jesus and think about it, we must open our mouths and speak it out loudly over our situation; "the blood of Jesus, the blood of Jesus, the blood of Jesus". We must shout this out until the demons go. We must also press our victory over the darkness until we are confident that our success is settled in heaven, in earth, and in hell. Do not stop short of the goal post, the enemy will cut in on us; plead the blood of Jesus until the matter is completely resolved.

In Acts chapter 8 the bible says that the church was under persecution, which sent the apostles on their way to do what God had given them to do: to preach the gospel in all the world.

Philip went down to Samaria and preached Christ unto the people. Every time the church calls the name of Christ [the anointed one] it reminds the devil of Calvary; it reminds him and his cohorts that Jesus shed his blood for the sins of the world. The blood speaks when we call the name of Jesus Christ and the reality of defeat is obvious to the Lord's enemies.

Down in Samaria the people were bound with diseases: some had palsies and many were lame, others were possessed with unclean spirits. The name of Jesus reminded these evil spirits and the diseases, that the blood of Jesus had been shed and the price paid for their deliverance.

Jesus took his blood into the holiest, and all heaven was therefore ready to fight for the people, holding up the legal rights for their release.When Philip spoke the name of Jesus [whose blood has been shed] here is what happened: Acts 8:7-8 7. For unclean spirits, crying with loud voice came out of many that were possessed with them and many taken with palsies, and that were lame, were healed. 8. And there was great joy in that city.

In St John 6:63 the word states that, Except ye eat the flesh of the Son of man and drink his blood, ye have no life in you. When man sinned at the beginning, the life of God went out of him and he died. Genesis 2:17 But of the tree of the knowledge of good and evil, thou shalt not eat of it, for in the day that thou eatest thereof thou shalt surely die. Since the blood of calves and of goats could not remove sin so that man could regain life, Jesus had to pour out his blood and give it to man to drink, in order to put life back into him.

How can I apply the blood of Jesus to regain life?

I will go a step further. When you read the word of God, eat it. How? Meditate upon it until it begins to open up with revelation. That is eating Jesus' flesh [food]. The word of God is food for the hungry soul. When we plead the blood of Jesus, "the blood of Jesus, the blood of Jesus, the blood of Jesus" we are spiritually drinking the blood, we are pouring it into our inner man. The blood becomes alive in us and speaks.

In the realm of the spirit, the blood of Jesus is saying to satan and his demons, You are defeated and I am here to restore life to man so that he can have fellowship with Jesus. All demons must leave because the price for man's freedom has been paid by the blood of Jesus and legally man is now God's property. The blood cries out "Jesus Christ is Lord". That is why when we pleaded the blood of Jesus over our dead ones, they received life.

- **The blood heals**

Isaiah 53:5 But he was wounded for our transgressions, he was bruised for our iniquities: the chastisement of our peace was upon him; and with his stripes we are healed.

Leviticus 14: 5-7 [GNB] 5. Then the priest shall order one of the birds to be killed over a clay bowl containing fresh spring water. 6. He shall take the other bird, and dip it, together with the cedar-wood, the red cord, and the hyssop, in the blood of the bird that was killed. 7. He shall sprinkle the blood seven times on the person who is to be purified from his skin disease and then he shall pronounce him clean. He shall let the live bird fly away over the open fields.

According to Isaiah 53:5, out of the beatings come the healings. I often speak these words over people when I am praying to the Lord for their healing and I then begin to confess the blood of Jesus [the blood of Jesus, the blood of Jesus, the blood of Jesus]. The blood from Jesus' stripes answers: "They are no longer your property satan, Jesus' beatings have given them their healings, these souls are no longer yours. They have been purchased by Jesus, with his blood, now let them go". Jesus, by his blood heals nearly all the people we pray for, praise his holy name. We are more than conquerors through him that loved us [Romans 8:37].

The word tells in Leviticus 14:5-7 of the priest killing the live bird over a clay pot with water. We are God's vessels and we must have the water of the word in us that will receive the blood of Jesus to give us life. We also need to be dipped in the blood of Jesus to kill off the sin that is keeping us alive to satan's works of darkness.

The leprosy in our lives must be sprinkled with the blood of Jesus. Sprinkle the disease, the confusion, the poverty and lack, your disobedient children, your unsaved husband/wife, your job, your sleep; with the blood of Jesus. It makes all the difference. The blood will sanctify the matter, bring life to your dead condition and cause your difficulties to flee. Plead the blood of Jesus and send your troubles flying into the open fields, never to return. They will certainly get lost out there.

Call your disease by name [asthma, tumours, high blood pressure, diabetes, heart trouble, cancer, sickle cell disease, thrombosis, paralysis, heart condition etc.] and say, "I sprinkle you with the blood of Jesus and command you to flee, in the mighty name of Jesus". It surely works.

- **The blood gives peace**

Colossians 1:20 And having made peace through the blood of his cross, by him to reconcile all things unto himself; by him, I say, whether they be things in earth, or things in heaven.

Israel needed peace at a certain point in their history. There was going to be a giant to put down. The Lord knew this and had to elect the right man for the job; not without blood.

1 Samuel 16:1-5; 11-12 [GNB] 1. The Lord said to Samuel: How long will you go on grieving over Saul? I have rejected him as king of Israel. But now get some olive oil and go to Bethlehem, to a man named Jesse, because I have chosen one of his sons to be king. 2. How can I do that ? Samuel asked. If Saul hears about it, he will kill me!. The Lord answered; Take a calf with you, and say that you are there to offer a sacrifice to the Lord. 3. Invite Jesse to the sacrifice, and I will tell you what to do. You will anoint as king the man I tell you to. 4. Samuel did what the Lord told him to do and went to Bethlehem, where the city leaders came trembling to meet him and asked: Is this a peaceful visit Seer? 5. Yes, he answered, I have come to offer a sacrifice to the Lord. 11. Then he asked him, Have you any more sons? Jesse answered; There is still the youngest, but he is out taking care of the sheep. Tell him to come here, Samuel said. We wont offer the sacrifice until he comes. 12. So Jesse sent for him. He was a handsome, healthy, young man, and his eyes sparkled. The Lord said to Samuel, This is the one – anoint him! Samuel took the olive oil and anointed David in front of his brothers. Immediately the spirit of the Lord took control of David and was with him from that day on.

The blood had to be shed. The sacrifice had to be made before David could be anointed king. The blood pulls the anointing; after he was anointed with the oil by Samuel he was ready to serve God. It was war time and although a young boy, David was carrying the Lord's anointing.

The story of David and Goliath in 1 Samuel 17th chapter is a very wonderful story. It was war time and Jesse sent David to see how the battle was going and how his sons who were in the war were doing. The blood sacrifice was offered when David was chosen by the Lord to be king and the Lord's anointing was resting upon him.

David took to his brothers the food his father had given him for them. When he got to the camp he saw a lot of confusion and fear. Goliath the giant challenged Israel for 40 days. "Choose one of your men to fight me. If he wins and kills me, we will be your slaves, but if I win and kill him, you will be our slaves. Here and now I challenge the Israelite army. I dare you to pick someone to fight me!" When Saul and his army heard this they were terrified. [1 Samuel 17:8-11: GNB]. David looked at the situation and weighed it up. What will the king give to the man who kills this heathen giant and delivers Israel from such disgrace? David asked. The king has promised to give such a man a big reward; he will give this man his daughter to marry and his father will not have to pay taxes.

David's brother, Eliab, who was a soldier in the war overheard him asking questions and got angry with him. "You are only young and quite cheeky". Who is taking care of the sheep out in the wilderness? Do I not have a right to ask about the Lord's army? replied David. He had already decided that Goliath, an uncircumcised Philistine, should not be allowed to continue to defy the army of the Lord.

The soldiers who heard David speaking and saw his concern, told King Saul, who requested that David be brought to him. No one should be afraid of this uncircumcised Philistine, said David to the king. You are too young and inexperienced, and he is a man of war, replied King Saul. I killed a lion and a bear when they attacked the sheep, said David to the king. The Lord delivered me from them and he will deliver me out of the hand of Goliath. Put my armour on, said the king to David. David put them. I cannot wear them; I am not used to them.

The blood sacrifice was already offered and David had been anointed. He was ready for battle. He knew the battle was the Lord's When we are under the blood covering we are protected by the Lord and he will subdue all our enemies. How did David bring Goliath down? With a sling and five smooth stones. He discharged only one stone which the Holy Ghost took straight to Goliath's forehead and killed him. Zechariah 4:6 …It is not by might, nor is it by power; it is by the Spirit of the Lord.

The turmoil ended in the camp of the Lord when the man of God arrived who was covered under the blood and was carrying the anointing of the Lord. Peace came to the Lord's people. Yes, the blood brings peace.

CHAPTER 13

CLARIFYING WHAT THE BLOOD DOES FOR YOU – PART II

The blood cleanses
Leviticus 16:30; 1 John 1:7

The blood protects
Exodus 12:7, 13

The blood is covenant making
Exodus 24:3, 5-10

The blood cries and avenges
Genesis 4:8-11

- **The blood cleanses**

Leviticus 16:30 For on that day shall the priest make an atonement for you, to cleanse you, that ye may be clean from all your sins, before the Lord.

1 John 1:7 But if we walk in the light, as he is in the light, we have fellowship one with another, and the blood of Jesus Christ his Son cleanseth us from all sin.
In the record of Leviticus 16, the Lord appeared upon the mercy seat which was placed upon the ark in which was the Law of God. Aaron should not come before the mercy seat without the necessary requirements or he would die. Before he could appear before the mercy

seat, on which the Lord appeared in a cloud, Aaron, the high priest had to put on his proper garments after he had had his bath, and offered his bullock of the sin offering for himself and for his house. He had to be covered by the blood. To go within the veil in the presence of the Lord without the covering of the blood would expose his sins and show all his uncleanness and he would surely die. Before Aaron could atone for the sins of the people he and his family had to be cleansed from their sins. That is why we need to try and bring our families into the salvation of Jesus Christ when we become ministers of the Lord; plead the blood of Jesus over their lives and pray for them.

Aaron had to cleanse the tabernacle and everything in it including the altar with the bull's blood for himself and his family. He had to take two kids of the goats of the children of Israel and one ram for a burnt offering. He had to cast lots upon the two goats: one lot for the Lord, the other for the scapegoat. The goat upon which the Lord's lot fell was offered for a sin offering. He had to sprinkle the goat's blood to cleanse the place, as he did with the bull's blood. The cleansing with the goat's blood was on behalf of the people.

Leviticus 16:15-16 15. Then shall he kill the goat of the sin offering, that is for the people, and bring his blood within the veil, and do with that blood as he did with the blood of the bullock, and sprinkle it upon the mercy seat, and before the mercy seat: 16. And he shall make an atonement for the holy place, because of the uncleanness of the children of Israel, and because of their transgressions in all their sins: and so shall he do for the tabernacle of the congregation that remaineth among them in the midst of their uncleanness.

The blood of Jesus will clean out the church and your home. Plead the blood.

We can only walk in the light when we are clean. Satan and his works make us unclean and lead us into darkness. The good news is that we do not need to stay unclean because the blood of Jesus Christ, God's Son cleanses us from all sin [1 John 1:7]. Sin contaminates and defiles. It blocks our blessings, but if we apply the blood of Jesus we can be made clean.

- **The blood protects**

Exodus 12: 7,13 7. And they shall take of the blood and strike it on the two side posts and on the upper door post of the houses, wherein they shall eat it. 13. And the blood shall be to you for a token upon the houses where ye are; and when I see the blood, I will pass over you, and the plague shall not be upon you to destroy you, when I smite the land of Egypt.

Exodus 15:26 And said, If thou wilt diligently hearken unto the voice of the Lord thy God, and wilt do that which is right in his sight and wilt give ear to his commandments, and keep all his statutes, I will put none of these diseases upon thee, which I have brought upon the Egyptians: for I am the Lord that healeth thee.

God remembered his covenant with [Abram] Abraham to bring his descendants out of bondage and the time came when he had come down to deliver them. Genesis 15:13-14 13. And he said unto Abram, know of a surety that thy seed shall be a stranger in a land that is not theirs, and shall serve them; and they shall afflict them four hundred years. 14. And also that nation whom they shall serve, will I judge: and afterward shall they come out with great substance.

The book of Exodus chapters 1 to 12 gives us the full story of God's mighty hand upon the Egyptians and their king to release his people from their bondage. Only seventy people [Israel's family] went down to Egypt during the time of famine. Israel's son, Joseph, sold by his brothers, arrived in Egypt safely. God had placed him there to take care of his family in time of need. God's ways are past finding out. God took care of the whole family, including his young brother Benjamin and his father, whom Joseph had his older brothers bring down to Egypt. They were happy there. However, when Joseph died, the Pharaoh who reigned noticed God's blessings upon the Israelites and he did not like what he saw. The Israelites were numbering about half a million persons and he feared they might take over his country in time. He therefore made slaves of them.

God had a man prepared, to bring the Israelites out of their slavery [with the help of his brother], and he sent Moses and Aaron to command the Egyptian king to let the people go. Obviously, the slave labour was going well for the king and he was unwilling to release them to go and sacrifice to the Lord. Nine plagues swept through the land of Egypt by the mighty hand of God, ministered by his servants Moses and Aaron. The stubbornness of the hardened king brought down the righteous judgement of God. It was time to take his people out of bondage and the Lord's will be done.

The people were ordered by the Lord, through Moses and Aaron to choose either a lamb or a young goat for each household. [Your family is in this]. If the family was too small to eat a whole animal they should share it with the next door neighbour, in proportion to the number of people and the amount that each person could eat. The animal should be one year old, without defect.

The Lord would go through Egypt on the fourteenth night of the first month of the year and kill all the first-born males, both human and animal, and punish all the gods of Egypt. On that evening the Israelites should kill the animal and put the blood in a bowl. They should dip a sprig of hyssop in the blood and wipe the blood on the doorposts and on the beam above the door of the house. No one should leave the house. The destroying angel was assigned by the Lord to go through the land of Egypt and kill all the first-born males but when he saw the blood he would pass over those houses and no one in the houses with the blood mark would be killed.

The children of Israel did as they were commanded by Moses and Aaron and they were all safe in their houses, marked off by the blood. The blood was their protection. The whole family was protected.

Call your children in your house by pleading the blood of Jesus over them. By faith daub the blood of Jesus over the beams of your house and keep out those evil demons. The thief and robber must pass your house as you place the blood of Jesus over it. Jesus' blood is much more powerful than the blood of animals. They had the type in Egypt, we have the reality – Jesus the Lamb of God. St John 1:29 Behold the Lamb of God which taketh away the sin of the world.

The flesh of the animal represented the word of God. They were commanded to eat the flesh. St John 6:53

Then said Jesus unto them, Verily, verily, I say unto you, Except ye eat the flesh of the Son of man and drink his blood, ye have no life in you. They needed the life of God in them to make the journey. This would be forty years in the wilderness before they could enter the promised land. There would be many enemies in the way and many battles to be fought.

The blood is your protection. Cover your home and your family with it. Plead the blood of Jesus over your furniture, your motor car, your job, your finances, your food, your clothes. Plead the blood of Jesus over your food before you eat it and protect your stomach from food poisoning. The blood of Jesus is your protection. It works.

- **The blood is covenant-making**

Exodus 24:3, 5-10 3. And Moses came and told the people all the words of the Lord, and all the judgements; and all the people answered with one voice, and said, All the words which the Lord hath said, will we do. 5. And he [Moses] sent young men of the children of Israel, which offered burnt offerings and sacrificed peace offerings of oxen unto the Lord. 6. And Moses took half of the blood, and put it in basins; and half of the blood he sprinkled on the altar. 7. And he took the book of the covenant, and read in the audience of the people: and they said, All that the Lord hath said will we do, and be obedient. 8. And Moses took the blood and sprinkled it on the people, and said, Behold the blood of the covenant, which the Lord hath made with you concerning these words. 9. Then went up Moses, and Aaron, Nadab, and Abihu, and seventy of the elders of Israel; and they saw the God of Israel; and there was under his feet as it were a paved work of a sapphire stone, and as it were the body of heaven in his clearness.

Moses told the people all that the Lord had instructed him to advise them. I will mention a few:

- Do not spread false rumours, and do not help a guilty man by giving false evidence. [Exodus 23:1 GNB]

- Do not follow a multitude to do evil. [Exodus 23:2]

- Do not ill-treat a foreigner; you know how it feels to be a foreigner, because you were foreigners in Egypt. [Exodus 23:9 GNB]

- Do not bow down to their gods [the gods of the heathen nations] or worship them, and do not adopt their religious practices. Destroy their gods and break down their sacred stone pillars. [Exodus 23:24 GNB]

- If you worship me, the Lord your God, I will bless you with food and water and take away all your illnesses. [Exodus 23:25 GNB]

The people replied, "All that the Lord has spoken we will do". Saying that was not enough. The covenant between them and God had to be settled with blood. Moses, therefore sent young men to offer burnt offerings and sacrifice peace offerings of oxen unto the Lord.

Moses poured half of the animal blood in basins and half of the blood he sprinkled on the altar. Then he took the book of the covenant and read it to the people. Again they said, All that the Lord has said we will do and be obedient. Moses then sprinkled the people with some of the blood and said, Behold the blood of the covenant which the Lord has made with you concerning these words. God had promised to bless them if they obeyed his words and the people had agreed to be obedient. A covenant had been made and the covenant was sealed with blood.

Now, lift up the blood of Jesus and make a covenant with God to live for him completely and see how God will bless you. Remember it is the blood of Jesus which allows us access to the presence of God. We would not be allowed to make any covenant with God, if Jesus had not given us his precious blood and we must present the blood of Jesus in making our covenant with God.

Shout out, The blood of Jesus, and say, Lord, if you give me that job I will pay my tithes and give substantial offerings to support your work. Say, the blood of Jesus, the blood of Jesus. Lord, if you save my children, I will sacrifice time to work for you. Go on, plead the blood of Jesus, and say, Lord Jesus, if you take away barrenness from me I will give the child you give me back to you like Hannah did. 1 Samuel 1:27-28 27. For this child I prayed, and the Lord hath given me my petition which I asked of him. 28. Therefore also I have lent him to the Lord; as long as he liveth he shall be lent to the Lord.
Read the covenant book, the bible, and make covenants with God according to his word. You must take with you the blood of Jesus as you stand before the Lord. Exodus 15:26 And said, If thou wilt diligently hearken to the voice of the Lord thy God, and wilt do that which is right in his sight, and wilt give ear to his commandments, and

keep all his statutes, I will put none of these diseases upon thee which I have brought upon the Egyptians: for I am the Lord that healeth thee.

Now say: On the merits of the blood of Jesus, I covenant with you Lord to obey your word and receive healing of my diseases and I covenant with you to dedicate my life to love, serve, and obey you. Plead the blood of Jesus at the end of making this covenant. The blood seals the covenant. The blood of Jesus, the blood of Jesus, the blood of Jesus!

- **The blood cries and avenges**

Genesis 4:1-12 [GNB] 1. Then Adam had intercourse with his wife, and she became pregnant. She bore a son and said, By the Lord's help I have acquired a son. So she named him Cain. 2. Later she gave birth to another son, Abel. Abel became a shepherd but Cain was a farmer. 3. After some time, Cain brought some of his harvest and gave it as an offering to the Lord. 4. Then Abel brought the first lamb born to one of his sheep, killed it, and gave the best parts of it as an offering. The Lord was pleased with Abel and his offering, 5. But he rejected Cain and his offering. Cain became furious, and he scowled in anger.

6. Then the Lord said to Cain, Why are you angry? Why that scowl on your face? 7. If you had done the right thing, you would be smiling; but because you have done evil, sin is crouching at your door. It wants to rule you, but you must overcome it. 8. Then Cain said to his brother Abel, Let's go out in the fields. When they were out in the fields, Cain turned on his brother and killed

him. 9. The Lord asked Cain, Where is your brother Abel? He answered, I don't know. Am I supposed to take care of my brother? Then the Lord said, Why have you done this terrible thing? Your brother's blood is crying out to me from the ground, like a voice calling for revenge. You are placed under a curse and can no longer farm the soil. It soaked up your brother's blood as if it had opened its mouth to receive it when you killed him. 12. If you try to grow crops, the soil will not produce anything; you will be a homeless wanderer on the earth.

From the very beginning the lamb played a very important part in sacrificial offerings to the Lord. It is obvious the boys knew what God required as offerings. Cain was not prepared to go out of his way to give God the right offering. Possibly, he would have had to buy a lamb from his brother. He just did not bother. Although he knew what was required he gave what he had. Unfortunately, there was no blood to cover his sins.

Abel, however, gave God the first and best lamb born to one of his sheep. He killed it and gave the best parts of it to the Lord as his offering. This was a powerful type. This was a representation of "the Lamb of God" which would take away the sin of the world [St John 1:29]. The blood from the lamb covered Abel's sin and made him and his offering acceptable to the Lord. Blood was shed.

There will always be false brothers who will refuse to do what is right, who will disobey the Lord and give what they have instead of making an effort and taking the time to please the Lord. When the blessing does not come their way, they will get bitter and hate the ones who put in their best and please the Lord.

Instead of repenting and doing what was right in order to get the blessing, Cain rose up against his holy brother and killed him. However, he would not get away with his wickedness because blood cries and avenges. The life of the flesh is in the blood, and although Cain thought that was the end of his brother, his blood cried out to God from the ground where it was poured. The blood had life in it and was speaking to God. It was making the complaint that his brother had killed him. The blood of Abel was calling for vengeance from the Lord. The Lord heard the voice of the blood of Abel. God is much more likely to hear the voice of the blood of Jesus. That is why we should plead the blood of Jesus when people hurt us. Jesus' blood speaks better things than the blood of Abel. Hebrews 12:24 And to Jesus the mediator of the new covenant, and to the blood of sprinkling that speaketh better things than that of Abel. When satan and his co-workers come against you, plead the blood of Jesus and God will take vengeance in your behalf.

Down through the ages the earth has soaked up much blood, some innocent. I shudder to think of the cries of the blood that has gone up to God, and is still going up day by day.

Jesus' blood is the most powerful and its cries go to God as we plead it over our every circumstance and condition. Plead the blood of Jesus and praise the Lord.

Applications of the blood of Jesus

1. SPRINKLE IT
2. SHOUT IT OUT
3. STRIKE IT ON
4. DIP THINGS IN IT
5. POUR IT ON
6. DRINK IT

- **Sprinkle it**

Exodus 24:5-13; 1 Peter 1:2-5; Leviticus 16:11,14-15; Hebrews 9:13-14

Exodus 24:5-13 5.And he sent young men of the children of Israel, which offered burnt offerings and sacrificed peace offerings of oxen unto the Lord. 6. And Moses took half of the blood, and put it in basins, and half of the blood he sprinkled on the altar. 7. And he took the book of the covenant, and read n the audience of the people: and they said, All that the Lord hath said will we do and be obedient. 8. And Moses took the blood, and sprinkled it on the people, and said, Behold the blood of the covenant, which the Lord hath made with you concerning all these words. 9. Then went up Moses, and Aaron, Nadab and Abihu, and seventy of the elders of Israel. 10. And they saw the God of Israel: and there was under his feet as it were a paved work of a sapphire stone and as it were the body of heaven in his clearness. 11. And upon the nobles of the children of Israel he laid not his hand: also they saw God, and did eat and drink. 12. And the Lord said unto Moses, come up to me into the mount, and be there: and I will give thee tables of stone, and a law, and commandments which I have written; that thou mayest teach them. 13. And Moses rose up, and his minister Joshua, and Moses went up into the mount of God.

1 Peter 1:2-5 2. Elect according to the foreknowledge of God the Father, through sanctification of the Spirit, unto obedience and sprinkling of the blood of Jesus Christ: Grace unto you, and peace be multiplied. 3. Blessed be the God and Father of our Lord Jesus Christ, which according to his abundant mercy hath begotten us again unto a lively hope by the resurrection of Jesus Christ from the dead. 4. To an inheritance incorruptible, and undefiled and that fadeth not away, reserved in heaven for you. 5. Who are kept by the power of God through faith unto salvation ready to be revealed in the last time.

Leviticus 16:11, 14-15 11. And Aaron shall bring the bullock of the sin offering, which is for himself, and shall make an atonement for himself, and for his house, and shall kill the bullock of the sin offering which is for himself. 14. And he shall take of the blood of the bullock and sprinkle it with his finger upon the mercy seat eastward, and before the mercy seat shall he sprinkle of the blood with his finger seven times. 15. Then shall he kill the goat of the sin offering, that is for the people, and bring his blood within the vail, and do with that blood as he did with the blood of the bullock and sprinkle it upon the mercy seat, and before the mercy seat.

Hebrews 9:13-14 13. For if the blood of bulls and of goats, and the ashes of an heifer sprinkling the unclean, sanctifieth to the purifying of the flesh: How much more shall the blood of Christ, who through the eternal Spirit offered himself without spot to God, purge your conscience from dead works to serve the living Glod.

- **Shout it out – It cries**

Genesis 4:4-10 4. And Abel, he also brought of the firstlings of his flock and of the fat thereof. And the Lord had respect unto Abel and to his offering. 5. But unto Cain and to his offering he had not respect. And Cain was very wroth and his countenance fell. 6. And the Lord said unto Cain, Why art thou wroth? And why is thy countenance fallen? 7. If thou doest well, shalt thou not be accepted? And if thou doest not well, sin lieth at the door. And unto thee shall be his desire, and thou shalt rule over him. 8. And Cain talked with Abel his brother: and it came to pass, when they were in the field, that Cain rose up against Abel his brother, and slew him. 9. And the Lord said unto Cain, Where is Abel thy brother. And he said, I know not: Am I my brother's keeper? 10. And he said, What hast thou done? the voice of thy brother's blood crieth unto me from the ground. [The blood has a voice, to cry!].

- **Strike it on your houses**

Exodus 12:4-7, 13-14 4. And if the household be too little for the lamb, let him and his neighbour next unto his house take it according to the number of the souls; every man according to his eating shall make your count for the lamb. 5. Your lamb shall be without blemish, a male of the first year ye shall take it out from the sheep, or from the goats. 6. And ye shall keep it up until the fourteenth day of the same month: and the whole assembly of the congregation of Israel shall kill it in the evening. 7. And they shall take of the blood, and strike it on the two side posts and on the upper door posts of the houses, wherein they shall eat it. 13. And the blood shall be to you for a token upon the houses where ye are: and when I see the blood, I will pass over you, and the plague shall not be upon you to destroy you, when I smite the land of Egypt. 14. And this day shall be unto you for a memorial; and ye shall keep it a feast to the Lord throughout your generations: ye shall keep it a feast by an ordinance for ever.

We must keep using the blood of Jesus for ever. In Moses' dispensation it was a shadow. In the dispensation of Christ [New Covenant] it is a reality.

Do you want the disease germs to disappear from your house? Strike on the blood.

- **Dip things in it**

Exodus 12: 22-24 22. And ye shall take a bunch of hyssop and dip it in the blood that is in the basin, and strike the lintel and the two side posts with the blood that is in the basin; and none of you shall go out at the door of his house until the morning. 23. For the Lord will pass through to smite the Egyptians; and when he seeth the blood upon the lintel and on the two side posts, the Lord will pass over the door, and will not suffer the destroyer to come in unto your houses to smite you. 24. And ye shall observe this thing for an ordinance to thee and to thy sons for ever.

We must get our children saved because the blood is for us and for them for ever. They too must take advantage of the blood and use it. The blood is for all time, to keep the destroyer away from us. Dip your family in it, dip your job in it, dip your finances in the blood, and praise the Lord for it. Dipping in the blood makes all the difference.

- **Pour it on**

Leviticus 8:13-15 13. And Moses brought Aaron's sons, and put coats upon them, and girded them with girdles, and put bonnets upon them, as the Lord commanded Moses. 14. And he brought the bullock for the sin offering: and Aaron and his sons laid their hands upon the head of the bullock for the sin offering. 15. And he slew it; and Moses took the blood, and put it upon the horns of the altar round about with his finger, and purified the altar, and poured the blood at the bottom of the altar and sanctified it, to make reconciliation upon it.

Pour the blood in every room in your house and sanctify them, then praise the Lord.

Exodus 29: 10-12 10. And thou shalt cause a bullock to be brought before the tabernacle of the congregation: and Aaron and his sons shall put their hands upon the head of the bullock. 11. And thou shalt kill the bullock before the Lord, by the door of the tabernacle of the congregation. 12. And thou shalt take the blood of the bullock, and put it upon the horns of the altar with thy finger, and pour all the blood beside the bottom of the altar.

Pour out all the blood at the place of prayer. You will become a prayer warrior. Praise the Lord.

- **Drink the blood**

St John 6:53-56 53. Then Jesus said unto them, Verily, verily, I say unto you, Except ye eat the flesh of the Son of man, and drink his blood, ye have no life in you. 54. Whoso eateth my flesh and drinketh my blood, hath eternal life; and I will raise him up at the last day. 55. For my flesh is meat indeed, and my blood is drink indeed. 56. He that eateth my flesh and drinketh my blood, dwelleth in me, and I in him.

Begin to drink blood: Yes, drink the blood of the Lord Jesus Christ.

Regarding the application of the blood of Jesus:

How do I: **Sprinkle it; Shout it out; Strike it on; Dip things in it; Pour it on; Drink it?**

Sprinkle it: Stand on your feet and by faith, take hold of a bucket in your hand. Now fill your hand with that blood and walk around wherever you want the blood to break satan's chains, and sprinkle the blood. As you do this say: the blood of Jesus, the blood of Jesus, the blood of Jesus. I sprinkle this place [or people] with the blood of Jesus.

You should sprinkle anything that is a problem to you.

Shout it out: You are witnessing an accident, or something really terrible is happening, cry out loud: the blood of Jesus, the blood of Jesus, the blood of Jesus. Shout it out.

Strike it on: Get, by faith, a large brush, hold the handle and by faith dip it in that basin of Jesus' blood and get out there, at the front of your house and strike on the blood on the door posts, the lintels etc. You should strike on the blood of Jesus wherever it is necessary.

Dip things in it: I get a full basin of Jesus' blood [by faith] and I dip all members of my family in it. In fact, I very often call a sea of blood to come and I bathe my family in it. For divine protection, dip whatsoever you need protected in the blood of Jesus. Once they are wet with the blood of Jesus, no devil/demons or evil circumstances can touch them.

Pour it on: Take your basin of Jesus' blood and physically walk to the family altar in your home and pour out the blood on that altar to purify and cleanse it and to drive away the demons. As you pour the blood on say: "the blood of Jesus is purifying this altar and driving away the demons". Prayer then becomes a mighty ministry and the blood of Jesus a powerful weapon to give us the victory.

Do the same in the house of God. The church then becomes a fire house of prayer where you will witness signs and wonders and mighty deeds.

Drink it: Take hold of a cup of cold/warm water and begin to drink it slowly. As you do this say: I drink the blood of Jesus, I drink the blood of Jesus. You can also put an empty cup to your mouth and say: Lord fill this cup with Jesus' blood; and then drink from it by faith. These things do take place in the spirit realm as you do them by faith in the natural realm.

As you minister in this way the anointing of God will come upon your life. Whenever I use the blood of Jesus I feel the powerful presence of the Lord and I use the blood of Jesus in every condition of life. It works every time, praise the Lord.

Now you know what to do, go and do it. Luke 10:37 .....Then said Jesus unto him, Go and do thou likewise.

CHAPTER 14

MORE TESTIMONIES

J R's Testimony

I was not a Christian at the time I listened to a gospel cassette tape from a Sunday morning radio ministry of Apostle Lake and the apostolic team.

I went to the hairdresser's as usual to have my hair done. She was playing a gospel cassette tape from one of the Sunday morning broadcasts. Apostle Lake prayed and before ministering the word of God she asked the listeners to pray repentance prayers. She spoke the words and asked the listeners to repeat after her. She then began to plead the blood of Jesus, saying: the blood of Jesus, the blood of Jesus, the blood of Jesus. In fact, she said these words many times, after which she began to minister healing. "Someone is listening who has a terrible pain in her back, Apostle Lake said: Put your hand at the place where the pain is and say: On the merits of the blood of Jesus shed for me, I command you pain to disappear. The reason for the pain must go as well".

At the time I had the most excruciating pain in my back and I grabbed hold of the opportunity to be healed. I placed my hand on the area where the pain was and sure enough the pain disappeared, and I was completely healed. I rang Apostle Lake and gave her my testimony. She prayed for me over the telephone; I submitted my life to the Lord and will be attending the church services.

A point of note: Apostle Lake quoted healing scriptures:

Isaiah 53:5 But he was wounded for our transgressions, he was bruised for our iniquities: the chastisement of our peace was upon him; and with his stripes we are healed.

Exodus 15:26 If thou wilt diligently hearken unto the voice of the Lord thy God, and wilt do that which is right in his sight, and wilt give ear to his commandments, and keep all his statutes, I will put none of these diseases upon thee, which I have brought upon the Egyptians: for I am the Lord that healeth thee.

The Lord has added another member to Apostle Lake's ministry.

Sister J's testimony

I am a Christian. My husband died a few years ago and on and off I have suffered from mild depression. There were times when I felt very low.

One Sunday morning I decided to turn on my radio whilst doing the cooking and listen to a Christian broadcast. I turned the radio on and began to search for a Christian programme. I heard some preaching on the blood of Jesus and I listened. The ministry was very powerful and in my Christian walk I had not heard preaching like that on the blood of Jesus. I was very blessed and I seemed to have learned a lot in such a short time. My depression seemed to have lifted and I felt very happy.

At the end of the studies/preaching, Apostle Lake ministered to the needs of the listeners. She asked them to pray repentance prayers and she ministered the blood of Jesus to drive away any unclean spirits that held the people captive. She asked the listeners to help her in pleading the blood of Jesus. She told them to place one hand on their problem and the other on the radio. She told the people that if the problem was something they could not place their hand on, they should place that hand on their forehead. Apostle Lake commanded all spirits of infirmity to go, including all spirits of oppression and depression. After the ministration I felt much better and quickly wrote down the address of the church and the phone numbers given. The Thursday evening prayer house at Stockwell Park was a must for me.

I now attend nearly all the meetings. However, recently, I was not feeling very well. I have been planning to move house and the pressure of everything seemed to have got me down. I telephoned Apostle Lake and poured out my heart. She prayed for me over the telephone, taking authority over every spirit of confusion, oppression and depression. She bound all the evil spirits in the name of Jesus and she pleaded the blood of Jesus. I pleaded the blood of Jesus with her, in agreement.

I was so unhappy about my condition, I had not eaten anything. However, after Apostle Lake had finished her phone call, I vomited out so much yellow phlegm, it would have to be seen to be believed. Some of it was in lumps. Since then I have felt like a weight has been lifted out of my body and I feel very well and I am rejoicing.

In all my years as a Christian, I have never heard the blood of Jesus ministered in this way, but it works.

Bless the Lord O my soul and all that is within me, Bless his holy name. Bless the Lord O my soul and forget not all his benefits Who forgiveth all thine iniquities; who healeth all thy diseases. [Psalm 103:1-3]

Apostle Lake's ministry has really helped me and I am staying with it. God bless you.

Brother H's testimony
[paraphrased]

Praise the Lord. As a Christian, I belonged to one of the mainstream churches but attended various ministries in the hope that someone, somewhere, might be able to help me.

I was a businessman in the property market. I was doing very well indeed until I met someone who talked me into investing in overseas business. He was from one of the developing countries where people are extremely crooked. Unfortunately, I fell for this man's smooth talk and started parting with thousands of pounds. I found out he was not alone but that it was a syndicate. There were times when I was asked to send thousands of pounds overseas to boost the business. This was going on for years and there was always a good reason why the business was not yielding profits and why it was necessary for me to invest more money.

As time went on I suspected that I had been "taken for a ride", although by then I was tens of thousands of pounds worse off. When I began to question things I realized I had some formidable enemies who were con-men and that my life could be in danger. Besides being very worried, I did not know how to get rid of them and they kept asking for money.

At nights demons began to visit me. My sleep went from me and I felt unwell. I spoke to my mother who was a Christian. She invited me to her church for help. I surrendered my life to the Lord. The ministers prayed for me but there was no change in my condition. I visited various ministries but there was no change; witchcraft was involved.

When my enemies found out that I was getting wise to who they were they sent demons to torment me in order to break me down, because I began to be unwilling to part with any more money. Much of my money was taken by these con-men and now I was under attack by unclean spirits. My marriage broke down and I lost my wife and children. I was desperate and visited the meetings of a few television evangelists. They were unable to help me.

It was a Wednesday evening. Apostle Lake was ministering on television. She testified of how God brought her son back from the dead as she pleaded the blood of Jesus. I became very hopeful, took her phone number and rang her. She took my details, prayed and encouraged me and then invited me to the church services. At the time she had started a prayer house in Stockwell, South West London. She informed me of the details of this and I promptly attended on the Thursday evening.

I arrived early at the prayer meeting. I had never heard prayers like those before. They were warfare prayers I was told. At the end of the prayer meeting an invitation was made to all those who needed special prayers. Needless to say, I went for prayers. Firstly she asked me what my problems were. I began to outline my story as follows:

- I have been conned by wicked men who had depleted my finances,
- Witchcraft had been placed upon my life so that I felt very miserable, lacked sleep and was unable to work,
- Demons tormented me during the day and even more so when I tried to sleep at night,
- I felt I was sitting on something fairly often, which seemed very real,
- I felt very confused, tired and tormented, although before all this took place I was very successful in my business and never had money problems,
- I was living with my elderly mother who, although a Christian and very sympathetic, did not understand the extent to which I was suffering,
- I was very unhappy.

By the time I had got this far, Apostle Lake stopped me and began to plead the blood of Jesus. She was binding those evil demons, and other ministers pleaded the blood of Jesus loudly and authoritatively. I felt much better as they pleaded the blood of Jesus and I also felt a release in my body.

Apostle Lake told me I needed to attend deliverance prayers on Wednesday evenings. She would need to get to the root of my problems and break the relevant curses.

This could take up to six weeks and all the areas of my life that had been affected would be dealt with. I went through the course of prayers. I noticed that the ministers who worked in the deliverance team all pleaded the blood of Jesus as they ministered to the people.
The blood of Jesus was a real tool against the devil during my deliverance prayers.

At the end of the prayers things miraculously took a turn for the better, I felt good. The demons went and I could sleep in peace. I started working again, bought a home and I am now a part of the Apostolic Church of God 7th Day ministries.

My problems have taught me to read my bible and pray and I have been drawn closer to the Lord by his Spirit.

I thank the Lord with all my heart, and I praise his holy name.

Sister E's testimony

I am from a family of diabetics. My mother had died from the disease and my younger sister had died from the disease when she was only 51 years old. At the age of 41 the doctors diagnosed that I also had the disease. Obviously, I was very worried and thought I would probably die from it as well. As the years went by, my condition worsened and my eyesight became very poor. I went to the opticians who sent me to the doctor. I was already under the treatment of the hospital doctors. Tests were carried out and glaucoma was diagnosed.

As a qualified nurse working on hospital wards over many years, I have seen the result of certain diseases.

The drugs I was given for the glaucoma and for my diabetes did not seem to help and the doctors feared what I feared, that I may end up becoming blind.

One of my sisters had been very ill for nearly 19 years. She had had some six operations and was bound to a wheelchair. She was in constant pain and the doctors could do no more for her.

She was listening to a radio broadcast one Sunday morning by Apostle Lake. She mentioned as she preached the word of God that there were some of the listeners who were so ill they were as good as dead. She said there was a crusade to be held where people could come and have their needs met by the Lord Jesus. My sister was taken there and received prayer. She later attended one of the church services where Apostle Lake and other ministers prayed for her and pleaded the blood of Jesus over her and she received a miracle.

My sister told me that she felt hands physically operating on her. The power of God had thrown her on the floor after she had been prayed for, and whilst she was on the floor, she felt herself being operated on and parts being put in her body. Whatever happened, when she got up off that floor, she was completely healed. A notable miracle had taken place.

"Come and receive your healing" she said. I was sceptical and would not attend the meetings for a while. However, one Sabbath, on my way to work, I thought about getting healed. I turned my car around and went to the church. Prayer time came and I went up for prayer. Apostle Lake prayed for me and pleaded the blood of Jesus. I had never experienced anything like that before.

[I was attending one of the main-stream churches where this was not done]. However, I just needed to be healed. Apostle Lake told me to go back to the doctors and return with my testimony. I did as she said. The doctors examined me and wondered what had happened. Remembering that the drugs were no longer working, they asked me what had taken place in my life. I told them that I had received prayer for my condition. They told me the glaucoma had been much improved and the diabetes was under control. I was relieved.

I went back to church with my testimony. Apostle Lake said that God did not do half jobs and she needed to hear that I was completely healed. She prayed for me again and pleaded the blood of Jesus. [The church also pleaded the blood of Jesus]. I have never heard it like that anywhere else, but it works miracles. She told me to go back to the hospital for my check-up and come back with my testimony. My next check-up was six months away. I went to the hospital at the appointed time and had the tests done as usual. The doctors seemed puzzled. The glaucoma had disappeared, my sight was perfect; I did not need glasses any more and there was no more diabetes. I was overjoyed.

I went back to church and testified of God's miracle-working power and we all rejoiced and gave God thanks for Jesus and his precious blood.

Satan was upset The devil was not very happy and decided to attack me again. I was driving to work as usual but found that I was not seeing properly. I managed to drive to the house of the patient I was going to see . [I am a district nurse]. My sight had become so bad that my husband had to come and take me home. I went back to church and told my problems to Pastor Judy Fullerton and herself and Evangelist Blake prayed for me, pleading the blood of Jesus. They ministered to me with all their heart, whilst the whole congregation pleaded the blood of Jesus. The power of the Lord threw me on the floor; the Lord dealt with me and when I got up I was completely healed. My sight had returned. Today I can see clearly without the use of glasses.

The medical profession is wonderful but they could not deny that something wonderful had taken place in my life. Jesus had healed me completely.

Thank God for the blood of Jesus, there is wonder working power in the blood. I can recommend the application of the blood of Jesus in every condition of life. It really works. Thank you Jesus, to you be all the praise and all the glory.

SCRIPTURE VERSES FOR YOUR TIME OF NEED

Psalm 107:19-20 19. Then they cry unto the Lord in their trouble and he saveth them out of their distresses. 20. He sent his word and healed them and delivered them from their destructions.

Isaiah 43:1-2 1. But now thus saith the Lord that created thee, O Jacob, and he that formed thee, O Israel, Fear not: for I have redeemed thee, I have called thee by thy name; thou art mine. 2. When thou passest through the waters, I will be with thee; and through the rivers, they shall not overflow thee; when thou walkest through the fire, thou shalt not be burned, neither shall the flame kindle upon thee.

Psalm 54:7 For he hath delivered me out of all trouble; and mine eye hath seen his desire upon mine enemies.

Jeremiah 32:17-19 17. Ah Lord God! Behold thou hast made the heaven and the earth by thy great power and stretched out arm, and there is nothing too hard for thee: 18.Thou shewest lovingkindness unto thousands, and recompensest the iniquity of the fathers into the bosom of their children after them: the Great, the Mighty God, the Lord of hosts, is his name. 19. Great in counsel and mighty in work: for thine eyes are open upon all the ways of the sons of men; to give every one according to his ways, and according to the fruit of his doings.

Nahum 1:7-9 [GNB] 7. The Lord is good; he protects his people in times of trouble; he takes care of those who turn to him. 8. Like a great rushing flood he completely destroys his enemies; he sends to their death those who oppose him. 9. What are you plotting against the Lord?

He will destroy you. No one opposes him more than once.

Mark 11:22-24 22. And Jesus answering saith unto them, Have faith in God. 23. For verily I say unto you, That whosoever shall say unto this mountain, Be thou removed, and be thou cast into the sea; and shall not doubt in his heart, but shall believe that those things which he saith shall come to pass; he shall have whatsoever he saith. 24. Therefore, I say unto you, what things soever ye desire, when ye pray, believe that ye receive them, and ye shall have them.

Luke 1: 37 For with God nothing shall be impossible.

Acts 3: 6-7 6. Then Peter said, Silver and gold have I none, but such as I have give I thee: In the name of Jesus Christ of Nazareth rise up and walk. 7. And he took him by the right hand, and lifted him up: and immediately his feet and ancle bones received strength.

Hebrews 12:2 Looking unto Jesus, the author and finisher of our faith; who for the joy that was set before him endured the cross, despising the shame, and is set down at the right hand of the throne of God.

Luke 10:18-19 18 And he said unto them, I beheld satan as lightening fall from heaven. 19. Behold, I give unto you power to tread on serpents and scorpions, and over all the power of the enemy: and nothing shall by any means hurt you.

Isaiah 45: 5, 7 5. I am the Lord and there is none else, there is no god beside me: I girded thee though thou hast not known me. 7. I form the light and I create darkness: I make peace and create evil: I the Lord do all these things.

Psalm 47:1 O clap your hands, all ye people: shout unto God with the voice of triumph.

CONCLUSION

Praise the Lord

I believe I have dug into many areas of the work of Christ's blood that I had not gone into before, and I feel that God will bring revelation to his church that she has not had before.

As the church moves on, we need the application of the blood of Jesus in every area of our ministry to remind the devil and his demons that the price for man's redemption has been paid. Every time we plead the blood of Jesus, the devil and his demons are being told that the battle for man's liberation has been fought and won by the Lord Jesus Christ and they are under our feet. They are being told in tones clear and loud that success and victory is ours through Jesus Christ our Lord. I believe we are hitting satan and the hierarchy of hell with force when we say: the blood of Jesus, the blood of Jesus, the blood of Jesus. We are pushing the point of their defeat home. They therefore tremble and fear because they become fully aware that the once blind, bound and frightened people he had under his iron rule are now God's weapons against his kingdom of darkness.

The blood of Jesus releases the captives and as we say the words: the blood of Jesus; chains are loosed, prison doors are opened and the souls of men are set free.

When we plead the blood of Jesus, the whole story of man's redemption unfolds and the following scripture rushes into the mind of God's arch-enemy:

Revelation 5:3-5 3. And no man in heaven, nor in the earth, neither under the earth, was able to open the book, neither to look thereon. 4. And I wept much, because no man was found worthy to open and to read the book, neither to look thereon. 5. And one of the elders saith unto me, Weep not: behold the lion of the tribe of Judah, the Root of David, hath prevailed to open the book, and to loose the seven seals thereof.

The devil thought there was no hope for man, but Jesus stood in our stead. He stepped forward, praise his holy name. The weight of sin to be carried for the whole world was so heavy in that book, no one could even so much as look at that book, but Jesus, yes, Jesus went forward for you and for me.

When we pour out the blood, the story says, the church under the leadership of Christ, is in control, it says we are more than conquerors through Christ's death on the cross.

We must wet everything with the blood of Jesus by pleading the blood of Jesus over everything we say and do and the demons will surely flee.

My prayer is that the Lord's church everywhere will receive revelation of the use of Christ's blood and will apply it to every situation. Remember, satan and his demons have contaminated almost everything, so plead the blood of Jesus over everything and the victory will be yours.

Every dead condition must respond to the voice of the blood of Jesus. Jesus said regarding Lazarus: Loose him and let him go [John 11:44]. When we say: the blood of

Jesus, we are pressing home the point: loose him and let him go in the name of Jesus. The chains will snap and the captive will be released.

Let us begin to use the blood of Jesus: Pour it out over relatives and friends, dip some in the blood of Jesus and wash off the drugs demons, pour it out at the family altar and get the family to pray, wash the grandchildren in the blood of Jesus and bring them under subjection to the word of God. Your prayer life will be full of the fire of the Holy Ghost when you get into the habit of pleading the blood of Jesus. Pour the blood of Jesus in every room in your home and wash out the Beelzebub flies, thus cleansing your home.

You have come into a higher level of truth revealed. Now, praise the Lord.

Psalm 113:1-3 1. Praise ye the Lord. Praise O ye servants of the Lord, praise the name of the Lord. 2. Blessed be the name of the Lord from this time forth and for ever more. From the rising of the sun unto the going down of the same the Lord's name is to be praised.

If there is any sickness in your body or your mind: Put your hand on the affected area and say: "You sickness [call it by name] I pour the blood of Jesus upon you and command you to die out of my body in the mighty name of the Lord Jesus Christ. I receive my healing on the merits of Christ's shed blood in Jesus' name. Now praise the Lord.

Psalm 111:1 Praise ye the Lord. I will praise the Lord with my whole heart, in the assembly of the upright, and in the congregation.

Finally, if you have read this far and you are still not saved, or you are backslidden, the blood of Jesus Christ will save you from all sin. Cry out, "God be merciful unto me a sinner and on the merits of the shed blood of Jesus Christ, please save me. Jesus, I confess you as Lord of my life. Thank you Jesus".

Now tell somebody you are saved and begin to attend a Holy Ghost, blood washed church in order that you may grow in the Lord.

I believe the Lord has blessed you in reading this book. I have written under the inspiration of the Holy Ghost. Testify what the Lord has done for you through reading this book and may the blessing of the Lord be yours in the precious name of Jesus.

Appendix 1

A FEW STEPS TO AID YOUR DELIVERANCE

*Repent and confess your sins before the Lord, on the merits of Christ's blood. Confess the sins of your mother's house and that of your father's house.

*Bind the strongmen holding you bound and drive them out with all their demons.

*Break unlawful sexual soul ties and demonic marriage bonds in the spirit realm.

*Destroy curses placed by witches and other evil people; break curses placed in your life by evil words by yourself or others.

*Break all spells and wash yourself and your family with the blood of Jesus. You must all drink the blood of Jesus by faith in Jesus' name.

*Plead the blood of Jesus aggressively over all your possessions and all who belong to you and seal them with the blood of Jesus, the fire of the Holy Ghost and ask the Lord to send guardian angels to protect his blessings on your life and that of your family.

*Ask the Lord for anointing upon you and yours for service in his kingdom.

Apostle Lake

Other books by the Author:

Christ's hand on my life
Why I despise witchcraft
And Various booklets

To contact the Author write to:

Apostolic Church of God 7th Day Ministries
P O BOX 304
Harrow
Middlesex
HA2 0UF
UK

e-mail: pastorlake@hotmail.co.uk

Website: www.acog7.org